# EVERY *CURSE* DESTROYED

# EVERY *CURSE* DESTROYED

**PASTOR DAVID RAMIAH**

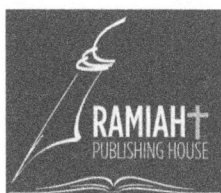

RAMIAH†
PUBLISHING HOUSE

**TORONTO CANADA**

**EVERY CURSE DESTROYED**
© David Ramiah 2018

Edited by Joy Hallwood
Final Edit by Patricia King-Edwards

This book is designed to provide accurate and authoritative information with regard to the subject matter covered. This information is given with the understanding that neither the author nor Christ Exalted Ministries is engaged in rendering legal, professional advice. Since the details of your situation are fact dependent, you should additionally seek the services of a competent professional.

Printed in Canada
March 2018

Ramiah Publishing House
22-90 Signet Drive,
Toronto, Ontario, M9L 1T5
www.DavidRamiah.com

Published in Canada
ISBN 978-0-9959385-3-3

Toronto Canada

# DEDICATION

*I dedicate this book to my Lord and Saviour, Jesus Christ.*

Other books by Pastor David Ramiah include

# SPECIAL THANKS TO:

This book would not be possible without the help of so many individuals who have read and given their opinions and thoughts on its content. I thank you all.

Thanks to my entire family, especially, my mom and dad who are always there for me.

A special thank you to Joy Hallwood, whose unwavering support and hard work never ceases.

And special thanks to Christ Exalted Ministries Congregation in Toronto.

*I love you all. God bless you.*

# CONTENTS

# EVERY *CURSE* DESTROYED

## PASTOR DAVID RAMIAH

*"Like a flitting sparrow, like a flying swallow, s
o a curse without cause shall not alight."*
Proverbs 26:2

# FOREWORD

What causes a believer to doubt the presence of the Lord in their life? Why is there this nagging feeling that God is not there, that He has left you to do your best on your own, under your own steam? When there are so many promises in Scripture regarding the Father's presence in our lives, through the power of the Holy Spirit, why do these feelings of despair and 'alone-ness' haunt the struggling believer's tattered spiritual life? Hosea says: "*My people are destroyed for lack of knowledge*"! (4:6)

This book, 'Every Curse Destroyed', delves into the misinterpretation surrounding the term 'generational curses', the spirit of abandonment and 'the orphan spirit' that are pervasive in the church today. The author weaves the Gospel message into the opening chapter, presenting a solid doctrinal basis from which he addresses the issue. The relationship to God as Father is crucial for the struggling believer to grab hold of. The ensuing chapters gently encourage the reader to solidify their original relationship with God by walking them through the logical progression of their initial faith commitment. In re-establishing and re-affirming this relationship, the believer has, through Christ, the beautiful imagery of 'adoption'. It becomes clear that we are no longer orphans and no longer under a curse. By skillfully linking the relevant Scriptures, Pastor David pulls together the penultimate facts of the relationship of a believer to their Heavenly Father, and further explains the truth behind the misconceptions and the faults of the erroneous teaching.

This is a wonderful book for the struggling believer, and, I believe, a great source of comfort for those who wish to mature spiritually. Pastors, Christian counsellors, and Spiritual Care workers will find this to be a very valuable resource for any personal library. I highly recommend it!

**Rev. Valda Douglas**
Hope For Today Fellowship
Ontario Bible Training Institute

# INTRODUCTION

Some years ago, something went terribly wrong in the Body of Christ. It adversely affected an entire multitude of people around the world. I have seen it in Canada, the United States of America, India, and Brazil. As well, I know that it is all over Europe and in other parts of the world — spreading like a disease. With the great speed and reach of the internet, any audience can be influenced and affected in seconds. Even prior to the internet, multitudes were quickly grabbed and swayed by television, radio, books and other media. It did not take long for it to have permeated all Christendom.

Sadly, all over the world, Christians are suffering a disastrous consequence of wrong teachings. This has kept many in bondage to this very day. Over the last thirty years, I have personally watched and listened to those who have been lured and led along the wrong path. They did not take the time to find out for themselves, if what they were learning was true or false. It was like a band wagon, or a passenger train giving free rides as everyone jumped on for the ride. Almost everyone climbed aboard, not paying attention or asking if the train was going in the direction that they wanted to go or should go. The train seemed to be heading in the right direction. For all intents and purposes, it was leaving from the correct station.

All that is needed is for one little mistake to take you totally away or further away from your true destination, cause you to lose time in the process, and sometimes lose a lot of money. A person can actually lose their entire livelihood with just the wrong set of information, and one bad decision. A trader in stocks and bonds has to only receive the wrong type or make of a product, one incorrect price calculation, or an incorrect time of sale, to lose millions in one trade.

How much are you yourself willing to gamble on receiving incorrect information versus receiving the true facts? Can you afford to lose say 5, 10, or 20 years of your life because you accepted the wrong lesson so that you put an error into practise, only to find out a long time later that it was not true? You may have tried and tried time and again. It seemed to work for a short time, but soon thereafter, you realized you were back to square one. Then you decided, "Well, I am used to this so I have to live with it. I can't change it anyway. I have lived like this all my life so I cannot get rid of it that easily. It's in my DNA, in my genes, from my forefathers, and I inherited it. I might as well learn to cope with it. One day, maybe, God will set me free."

However, my friends, God wants you free today! He desires for you to be free from anything and everything that Satan has brought upon you. God desires to liberate you from anything that you are struggling with, which you may believe you have inherited from your parents, or that you got hooked on to on your own.

I have been convicted for years that I am correct about the issues discussed in this book. However, I did not set out earlier to really press the point because I was not ready. Actually, I had hoped that someone else would have confronted the issue before me. Then I wouldn't have to. The thing is that when God gives you an assignment, it is yours. He does not take it back. It is yours to accomplish. You have to get it done. So, here I am setting out to bring you the truth that will set you free. I pray that the Lord will open your eyes, that He would give you the understanding you need, and that most of all, He will soften your heart to receive what He is saying to you today.

Thus, with the guidance and help of the Holy Spirit, and with all the hope in my heart to bring change into your life, I have diligently set out to put together in these pages what will help you to receive the truth and correct this error. I pray that the Biblical facts laid out in this book will bring a favorable transformation to you and to those around you.

I encourage you to be diligent, to pray and seek the help of the Holy Spirit, so that you may understand what is written herein, and grasp the truth that will set you free. My prayer is that light would be shed upon the dark areas and that things would become much clearer and brighter in the end.

God bless you.
**Pastor David Ramiah**

# 1

## ADOPTED

*"Having predestined us to adoption as sons by Jesus Christ to Himself, according to the good pleasure of His will."*
(Ephesians 1:5)

A man and his wife decided that they would have a child. They decided to adopt a son. So they set out to put in an application, and meet with the right government officials to set the process in motion. As the father waited, the excitement climbed. He got more and more eager every day. He could hardly wait for everything to be finalized. He wanted to take his new son home. Sometimes, his enthusiasm and excitement overwhelmed him, but he remained composed. Nevertheless, he just couldn't wait for it all to be completed. The process was very long, and drawn out. Finally, the wait ended. He became a father.

The young child was too little to recognize all that was happening to him. He did not realize that he was becoming a son to new parents. He was not aware that he had moved into a different home. He did not know that he had another mother and father somewhere out there, and that he had lived in their home prior to living in this one. Faces that he barely recognized were taking care of him now. Soon, though, he learned to love and trust them. All his needs were supplied. He had nothing to worry about. Whenever he needed something, these were the two people he would come to for help. He had no doubt that they would provide for him, protect him, and make sure that he was fine. He was soon calling them mom and dad.

Finally, he went to school. When his teacher called him by his first and last name, he promptly answered. He had no problem answering to his current name. After all, he did not know that he had had another name. No one had told him that he had had other parents. He did not know that he was adopted. His name was what it was, and he was who he was. Unless someone told him, this young boy would grow up and never know that he had been adopted. He would never come to know his past identity. To him, there was no other identity. In his heart, one day his dad would die and leave him an inheritance. This was his father. He didn't know any other. His dad was his dad. He knew full well that all that belonged to daddy would eventually become his. He was content.

## No other Inheritance Expected

There was only one thing that this adopted son would never expect, and that was, another inheritance from another set of parents. He didn't even know that they existed. Then again, *legally*, they were no longer his mom and dad. They, therefore, had no *legal* rights to him. The thought would never even enter into his mind that he could expect another heritage from anyone else. There wasn't any to expect or to have. As far as he was concerned, whatever his father left him -- that was his. Nothing more, nothing less... If someone had told him that he should expect something from someone else other than his parents, he would have thought that they were crazy and did not know what they were talking about. To expect to inherit something from another mom and another dad was absurd. It was absolutely ludicrous for him to expect some other inheritance from other parents.

## New Identity

Were you adopted? Like this young man, were you given a new name, a new home, and a new father?

Are you now called by your new name? What is it?

Have you moved out of your old home and now live in a new one?

What about your new father; who is he? What is his name?

Do you expect an inheritance from your new father?

What about your old father, are you going to inherit anything from him as well?

Who was your father before this?

Are you thinking what I am thinking? Do you see what I see? Can you picture yourself in your new home? Ah, you are thinking of Heaven. I am not thinking of that at all. I am not talking about the Celestial. Heaven is far away from what I am thinking about right now.

Permit me to share a little about myself. You see, the Bible tells me that I have been adopted into a new family. When I became born again, I received a new name. Today, I am called 'Christian'. In the past, I used to be called a 'Sinner'. Today, I live in a new home called 'the Body of Christ'. I no longer live in the same 'house' that I used to live in. Since the day I gave my life to Jesus Christ, I moved. As a matter of fact, the Bible tells me that *'I no longer live. It says that Christ lives in me'*. So, wow! I don't even live here. Oh, that's not all, I have a new Father. He is the same Father that my Lord and Saviour Jesus Christ has -- they call Him, 'God'. Do you know Him? Guess what? That's who my inheritance comes from.

What about my earthly dad? He has nothing to do with this! My heritage is not in him and does not come from him. The truth is that my earthly dad has also accepted Jesus Christ as Lord and Saviour. He, therefore, has the same Father as I do. Isn't that just amazing? Really, legally speaking, my earthly dad and I are brothers. Could anything be more awesome?

Yes, you see, my Heavenly Father is awesome and He does awesome, wonderful, and amazing things all the time. This is one of the best of them all as He made my earthly dad and me brothers. Therefore, my dad and I receive our inheritance from the same source, the same Father. Not from anyone else! Doesn't that wow you? It should.

## True Heritage

Since my earthly dad and I are brothers, I can't expect to inherit anything from him! He is my brother, not my father. He has nothing to do with passing on any real lasting heritage to me. Likewise, he does not have to expect an inheritance to be passed on to him from his own earthly father. Oh no, his father did not receive Jesus Christ as Lord and Saviour. You see, though, when my dad became born again, he changed fathers. He was adopted by God. God the Father became his Father. My earthly dad's heritage is totally from God the Father now. It is not from his earthly father who died a long time ago.

> *"Blessed be the God and Father of our Lord Jesus Christ, who has blessed us with every spiritual blessing in the heavenly places in Christ, just as He chose us in Him before the foundation of the world, that we should be holy and without blame before Him in love, having predestined us to adoption as sons by Jesus Christ to Himself..."* (Ephesians 1:3-5)

When Jesus Christ came into my heart by the Holy Spirit and I was born again -- my entire life changed. At that very moment, I was instantly, totally, and legally cut off from my earthly parents, from my grandparents, my great grandparents, and as far back as you wish to go. I was severed from them all. They are no longer legally my family. My family now is God's family. God took me into His house and into His family. He gave me His name, and sealed me with His Holy Spirit. I became His. I am now owned by God. No one else owns me or has legal rights to me like God does. *"But as many as received Him, to them He gave the right to become children of God, to those who believe in His name."* (John 1:12) *"The Spirit Himself bears witness with our spirit that we are children of God, and if children, then heirs—heirs of God and joint heirs with Christ ..."* (Romans 8:16-17)

Jesus Christ paid the full price in His death and resurrection for me. He bought me. I am His. He owns me. I cannot be claimed by another! Satan has no part in me. He has no legal rights to me. He cannot pass on to me anything from my ancestors. They are no longer my ancestors. They are not my family anymore. God's family is my family. God is my Father and my inheritance comes from Him. I am an heir of God, not of man! — I am a joint heir with Jesus Christ Himself.

> *"Therefore, if anyone is in Christ, he is a new creation; old things have passed away; behold, all things have become new. Now all things are of God, who has reconciled us to Himself through Jesus Christ, and has given us the ministry of reconciliation, that is, that God was in Christ reconciling the world to Himself, not imputing their trespasses to them, and has committed to us the word of reconciliation."* (2 Corinthians 5:17-19)

If you look closely, you will find that I carry the likeness and image of God my Father. Why? He enabled me to put on Christ. After I put on Christ through my new birth in Him, all things became new. I became new. I took on a new life with my Father God in His family, the Body of Christ.

*"For you are all sons of God through faith in Christ Jesus. For as many of you as were baptized into Christ have put on Christ. There is neither Jew nor Greek, there is neither slave nor free, there is neither male nor female; for you are all one in Christ Jesus."* (Galatians 3:26–28)

The truth is that my past is past. It is no longer part of me or my life. It has been left behind. That is why God says to me to forget the past because He has blotted out my sins and does not remember them anymore. Therefore, I must not allow myself to go back into my former life and relive what was previous. I must not dwell on what is gone. I have to go forward with Jesus Christ who is my strength, my life. No turning back, always pressing forward. *"Do not remember the former things, nor consider the things of old. Behold, I will do a new thing…"* (Isaiah 43:18, 19) God continued to say, *"I, even I, am He who blots out your transgressions for My own sake; and I will not remember your sins. Put Me in remembrance; let us contend together; state your case, that you may be acquitted."* (Isaiah 43:25, 26) If you are in Christ Jesus, you are a new creation in Christ -- the righteousness of God, royalty, a king and a priest, and a child of the Most High God

Dear God my Father, I thank You for adopting me into Your family and making me Your child. You have translated me into Your Kingdom and into Your light from a world of darkness, death and hell. I pray that by Your Holy Spirit, You will keep me in the light of Your Kingdom and that You will enable me to bring glory to your name. Thank You, Father. I ask this in Jesus' name. Amen.

# 2

## A NEW NAME

*"And I will make My covenant between Me*
*and you, and will multiply you exceedingly."*
(Genesis 17:5)

Long before God gave the law to Moses, God spoke to a man called Abram who lived in his father's house with his wife Sarai in a country called Ur. He was minding his own business and doing his own thing, when the Lord called him. God called Abram to walk with Him and made him a promise.

> *"Now the Lord had said to Abram, 'Get out of your*
> *country, from your family and from your father's*
> *house, to a land that I will show you. I will make*
> *you a great nation; I will bless you and make your*
> *name great; and you shall be a blessing. I will bless*
> *those who bless you, and I will curse him who curses*
> *you; and in you all the families of the earth shall be*
> *blessed. So Abram departed as the Lord had spoken*
> *to him..."* (Genesis 12:1-4)

Then God changed his name from Abram to Abraham, which is a shortened version of a Semitic phrase means Father of many nations; his wife's name was changed to Sarah.

It is important to note three specific things that took place. God made three demands of Abraham. One, he had to leave his father's house; two, he had to go away from his family; three, he had to leave his country. We must understand that these were not easy things to do. Abraham's father's house offered them protection. They had safety and security among his family. As well, there was food and a commonality in his country. However, in order for Abraham to become what God wanted him to be; he had to satisfy God's demands as they were linked to the great promise. What can we learn today from Abraham's obedience to these three requirements of God?

In these acts of obedience, we see separation. He was cut off -- a severance from his father, family and country. Thus, something very deep happened. From your father comes your name. From your family comes your identity. From your country comes your nationality. To obey the demands of God, Abraham had to lose all these -- his name, his family and his nationality. He would no longer receive help from his father. The protection and provision from his dad or his family would be severed. Very importantly, as well, he would no longer be influenced by his father's life. Further to this, he would no longer worship his father's 'god'. From the moment that Abraham obeyed the Lord, God our Father became his God and heavenly Father!

The Lord promised Abraham that He would give him his own house. He was not going to just receive his own house; though, God was going to make him a great nation. God would also make his name great. Thus, Abraham left his father's house, came out from under his father's influence, and went far away from every negative effect of his father's life. He departed from his father's family to make a family of his own. He also left his old country to obtain a country of his own. Abraham became a new man, and his descendants became a new people.

## Covenant

God always solidifies His agreement with man. He did it with Abraham.

> *"When Abram was ninety-nine years old, the Lord appeared to Abram and said to him, 'I am Almighty God; walk before Me and be blameless. And I will make My covenant between Me and you, and will multiply you exceedingly.' Then Abram fell on his face, and God talked with him, saying: 'As for Me, behold, My covenant is with you, and you shall be a father of many nations. No longer shall your name be called Abram, but your name shall be Abraham; for I have made you a father of many nations. I will make you exceedingly fruitful; and I will make nations of you, and kings shall come from you. And I will establish My covenant between Me and you and your descendants after you in their generations, for an everlasting covenant, to be God to you and your descendants after you. Also I give to you and your descendants after you the land in which you are a stranger, all the land of Canaan, as an everlasting possession; and I will be their God."* (Genesis 17: 4-8)

Then, God said to Abraham:

> *"As for you, **you shall keep My covenant, you and your descendants after you throughout their generations.** This is My covenant which you shall keep, between Me and you and your descendants after you: Every male child among you shall be circumcised; and you shall be circumcised in the*

*flesh of your foreskins, and it shall be a sign of the covenant between Me and you. He who is eight days old among you shall be circumcised, every male child in your generations, he who is born in your house or bought with money from any foreigner who is not your descendant. He who is born in your house and he who is bought with your money must be circumcised, and My covenant shall be in your flesh for an everlasting covenant. And the uncircumcised male child, who is not circumcised in the flesh of his foreskin, that person shall be cut off from his people; he has broken My covenant.' Then God said to Abraham, 'As for Sarai your wife, you shall not call her name Sarai, but Sarah shall be her name. And I will bless her and also give you a son by her; then I will bless her, and she shall be a mother of nations; kings of peoples shall be from her'.* " (Genesis 17: 5-16)

Abram received a new name, Abraham. No longer was he called or known by what his earthly father called him. He was now known by what his heavenly Father called him –Abraham. Then, Abraham received land:

*"On the same day the Lord made a covenant with Abram, saying: 'To your descendants I have given this land, from the river of Egypt to the great river, the River Euphrates— the Kenites, the Kenezzites, the Kadmonites, the Hittites, the Perizzites, the Rephaim, the Amorites, the Canaanites, the Girgashites, and the Jebusites.'"* (Genesis 15:18-21)

That name gave him a new identity. Abraham received a new name, got a new identity, a new family, a new country, became a new nation, a new people, and received a new inheritance.

God has the same for His children, His specially chosen, who have been saved and born again.

He gives us a new name –His own – 'Christian' and new identity just as Abraham received. He brings us into His new family for us and gives us a new country and a new nation – His Kingdom. We are thus a new people, who now receive a new inheritance. Are you ready?

If you haven't yet prayed the prayer of salvation, pray this from your heart. Invite Jesus Christ to be your Lord and Saviour. You will have a new life. The old one will be taken away. You will be able to live, move and have your being in Jesus. When you receive Him as your Lord and Saviour, His blood washes away all your sins. You are then presented totally clean, pure and holy to God, the Father. God becomes your Father. Go ahead and do it right now. It will be wonderful. I promise you.

> *"Dear God, I accept Jesus Christ as my Lord and Saviour. I repent of all my wicked ways. I renounce Satan and all his works. I am sorry for all the sins I have ever committed. Please forgive me and wash me with the blood of Jesus Christ, the Messiah, your Son, and make me totally clean. Please fill me with your Holy Spirit. Thank you for making me a brand new person today. I know that I will never ever be responsible for the sins of my forefathers. God, You are my Father now! My inheritance comes from You. And that inheritance is righteous. I ask all this in the name of Jesus Christ your Son, amen."*

# 3

## A NEW NATION

*"I will make you a great nation; I will bless*
*you and make your name great; and you shall*
*be a blessing."*
(Genesis 12:2)

Paul was so upset with Peter, the Apostle, who he confronted once in front of a whole crowd of people, about a particular situation. The Apostle, Paul, could not stand by and let things remain the way they were. He was fully persuaded and convinced in his heart regarding his understanding of the Scriptures. He also believed firmly that he had been given insight into things given to him by the Holy Spirit, that he tackled the situation head on. He could not allow them to continue in the manner in which they had been going. Sometimes, that is exactly how we need to be. Jesus did it!

When men gathered in the Temple of God and were trading and selling goods, Jesus got angry. He even got so angry that He chased them out of the Temple. He made a whip of cords and drove them right out of the House of God. No one could do or say anything to Him. Why? Because He was correct. The buyers and sellers knew that they had been doing wrong. Yet, the priests and the elders, who should have known better, stood still, said nothing, and did nothing. This wrong had continued to be practised in the temple itself for such a very long time, that it was commonly accepted by everyone. It didn't just happen overnight.

> *"Now the Passover of the Jews was at hand, and Jesus went up to Jerusalem. And He found in the temple those who sold oxen and sheep and doves, and the money changers doing business. When He had made a whip of cords, He drove them all out of the temple, with the sheep and the oxen, and poured out the changers' money and overturned the tables."*(John 2:13, 14)

Sometimes, you and I need to get angry just as Jesus did. Often, we are forced to respond to wrongs just as Jesus did. That's a good thing! Even though, some people may not like it. We have to stand up for what is right and good in the sight of God. People do not always accept what we say with open arms, but, if we are right about what we believe and God has convicted us about it, we must act. We must speak up.

Paul couldn't hold back. He had to act. He knew that he had to speak up. If he didn't, the wrong practice would have continued for years to come, and people would continue to be in bondage to the false teaching. He confronted Peter, who could not respond negatively to the truth because it was the truth. You cannot defeat the truth.

> *"Now when Peter had come to Antioch, I withstood him to his face, because he was to be blamed; for before certain men came from James, he would eat with the Gentiles; but when they came, he withdrew and separated himself, fearing those who were of the*

*circumcision. And the rest of the Jews also played the hypocrite with him, so that even Barnabas was carried away with their hypocrisy.*

*But when I saw that they were not straightforward about the truth of the gospel, I said to Peter before them all, 'If you, being a Jew, live in the manner of Gentiles and not as the Jews, why do you compel Gentiles to live as Jews? We who are Jews by nature, and not sinners of the Gentiles, knowing that a man is not justified by the works of the law but by faith in Jesus Christ, even we have believed in Christ Jesus, that we might be justified by faith in Christ and not by the works of the law; for by the works of the law no flesh shall be justified.*

*But if, while we seek to be justified by Christ, we ourselves also are found sinners, is Christ therefore a minister of sin? Certainly not! For if I build again those things which I destroyed, I make myself a transgressor. For I through the law died to the law that I might live to God.*

*I have been crucified with Christ; it is no longer I who live, but Christ lives in me; and the life which I now live in the flesh I live by faith in the Son of God, who loved me and gave Himself for me. I do not set aside the grace of God; for if righteousness comes through the law, then Christ died in vain.'"*
(Galatians 2:11-21)

What was this all about?

Well, Peter and some of the other apostles were teaching the Gentiles to live like the Jewish people. Gentiles are any non-Jewish people. Peter and the rest of the Jewish apostles wanted the Gentiles to practise the laws of the Jews. Basically, they were teaching a *new nation* of people to practise the laws of another nation. *Not only were they Gentiles, they were a "new nation" in Christ.* They were Christians.

They were from many different nations. As they became born again and joined the Body of Christ, they were no longer looked upon by the brethren according to what country they came from, or what nationality they were. As Christians, they became part of another Kingdom (God's), they received a new nationality, and were called by another name -- Christian. Similarly, you have become part of a 'new nation'. You are of God's Kingdom, and you are called by a new name -- Christian. There were certain laws and regulations practised by the Jewish Christians that Peter and others wanted the Gentile Christians to also practise. However, these observances which they performed were all fulfilled in Jesus Christ. Christians do not need to practise them, nor should they. Paul, therefore, demonstrated that the life of a Christian is one of faith and not of works.

## With Fear and Trembling

It is so important that we take every precaution to correctly interpret God's Word. So many could get hurt, led down a wrong path, robbed of their joy and peace, and suffer loss in many ways, if we do not.

> *"I marvel that you are turning away so soon from Him who called you in the grace of Christ, to a different gospel, which is not another; but there are some who trouble you and want to pervert the gospel of Christ. But even if we, or an angel from heaven, preach any other gospel to you than what we have preached to you, let him be accursed. As we have said before, so now I say again, 'if anyone preaches any other gospel to you than what you have received, let him be accursed.'"* (Galatians 1:6–9) *(Highlighted area, mine)*

God's Word is life. It gives life. If we would just stick to God's Word in our teachings, and with the help of the Holy Spirit understand fully what it says, we would not go wrong. If I am not sure what the Bible is saying to me about a particular matter; I leave it aside until I understand it fully. I wait for the Holy Spirit to interpret it for me and guide me into the truth of it. Even if I am convicted that I am right in my understanding of what I believe, I will not teach it until I am sure of it. This is why I am writing on this topic now. It has simmered in me for quite a while. So, my goal is to bring you the truth that will set you free. I pray that the Lord will open your eyes to understand and soften your heart to receive what He is saying to you today.

Paul further said, "*O foolish Galatians! Who has bewitched you that you should not obey the truth, before whose eyes Jesus Christ was clearly portrayed among you as crucified?*" (Galatians 3:1) Let us look closely and investigate this matter regarding curses, specifically, 'generational curses'. Let us not just skim over it or give it a quick glance, but let's pay close attention to it. Let us plead with the Holy Spirit to guide us and teach us that we may see the truth. That knowledge of the truth will set us free. Pray this with me:

> Dear Father, I am grateful to be called Your child. I am eternally thankful that You placed Jesus Christ on the cross to die to redeem me from sin and hell. Please illuminate my understanding to fully realize what You are saying to me, and lead me in all truth that I may not stray from the path of righteousness. I ask this in Jesus' name. Amen.

# 4

## THAT ORPHAN SPIRIT

*"I will not leave you orphans;*
*I will come to you."*
(John 14:18)

The fact is that 'an orphan spirit' has gone out into the world and is destroying countless numbers of Christians. It has been operating in the Body of Christ for decades now, perhaps, even for centuries. It is a spirit that is so masked and hidden under an exceptional cover, that it is not easily discovered. Jesus said, *"I will not leave you orphans; I will come to you."* (John 14:18) Something is being taught and has been taught for many years to the Body of Christ. It is so completely intertwined and subtle alongside other teachings that it is sometimes impossible for many people to distinguish between them. It is hardly noticed. Preachers preach it. Authors write about it. Teachers teach it, and none of them even realize that they have made a doctrine out of it. Thus, it lies there corrupting and debilitating Christians from all walks of life.

This orphan spirit and mentality has permeated the Kingdom of God. It is almost in every church. It has taken up its place in our homes, and schools, at work, and at our places of business. No one seems to acknowledge that it even exists. If you were to ask about it, you will more than likely get a definite answer like this, "No, I do not see an orphan spirit in the Church." Some may acknowledge that there is an orphan spirit operating in the Church, or that it is around, but they cannot point their finger at it.

It is so subtly hidden among the branches and the leaves that people do not recognize it. As it is so nicely disguised that it is almost impossible to separate it from among the barley and the wheat. At the bottom of people's plates, you will find that it has saturated right through their steaks and potatoes. Therefore, they have gullibly eaten it up, like candy given to children.

An orphan spirit is the agent for feelings of lack, abandonment and fatherlessness. It is the power behind the force of rejection, dejection, and discouragement. It is the same spirit that causes people to have low self-esteem, and be self-conscious. It pervades a feeling of being a slave or a lowly servant, and feelings of worthlessness; as if you are worth nothing and deserve nothing from God. These are all part of the influence and the work of this orphan spirit. This is the spirit that causes Christians to believe all untruths about themselves as children of God.

## Sonship

A relationship between a father and his child is very different from those of other relationships. There is a form of security in a good father that is not similar to the security one receives from others. There is a sense of going to dad when things go wrong and he will make it right. A consciousness exists that everything is all right when dad is around, but what if dad is not around? "Ah, but Pastor, God is my father." Is that really true? Is that how you really feel? Do you truly believe that? Then, why do you feel so terrible when some trouble arrives at your doorstep? Why do you sometimes want to give up on life and feel like no one cares for you and that He is not coming through for you? Why is it that you shout in despair, "Where are you God?" If you really believe that God is your Father, why do you not believe that He will come through for you?

An orphan spirit says, "God doesn't care about me. God has forgotten me. He does not think about me. He does not hear me. God is far away from me. He has left me to fight the battles alone." This evil spirit of hell marches on throughout Christendom, *"seeking whom he may devour"*. (I Peter 5:8) Sadly, enough, the multitude is already in his grip.

## Divide the Word

One of my greatest desires is that God's people would truly study their Bibles. My prayer is that they would seek the truth for themselves because it is as if their teachers are blind. It is as if they feed themselves and not the sheep. It is just as Jesus said, *"Let them alone. They are blind leaders of the blind. And if the blind leads the blind, both will fall into a ditch."* (Matthew 15:14) It is not God's desire that His people remain in bondage. It is not His desire that anyone remain with their eyes closed to the truth. He wants His people freed from this orphan spirit! There is only one way to be freed from it. *"And you shall know the truth, and the truth shall make you free."* (John 8:32) Only the living truth -- God's Word will set you free.

Dear friend, I am going to do due diligence to share truths with you in the treasure that you hold in your hands right now. I am going to rely fully on the Word of God and on the Holy Spirit to declare and demonstrate to you His revelations so that you may be totally free from this orphan spirit. What do many people do when they get paid? What do you do when you have money? Many people pay off their bills. They might buy groceries, nice clothes, shoes, or whatever else they may need. Others may put some in the bank as savings. Still others may even hide some in their home somewhere. Some people still do that, you know. Then, there are those others who first give their tithes and offerings to the church; then, go out to make their above purchases.

The Bible says that money answers everything. Truly it does. When you have enough of it, it takes care of all your needs and more. You have to have money to live debt free, pay your bills, and buy the things you need. Don't you? *"A feast is made for laughter, and wine makes merry; but money answers everything."* (Ecclesiastes 10:19). It is the same with God's Word. You have to receive the truth of God's Word to set you free, from the deception that has been taught for decades from pulpits, books, videos, and television. It is when you know the truth that you are set free.

The Bible says, *"Be diligent to present yourself approved to God, a worker who does not need to be ashamed, rightly dividing the word of truth."* (II Timothy 2:15) The Word of God will not rightly divide itself for you. It is your job and mine to open it up, search through it, and rightly divide it with the guidance of the Holy Spirit. If you are not doing that for yourself, Satan will continue to use teachers who will feed you leaven mixed in your dough, and you will forever remain in darkness to the truth. I do not believe, though, that anyone wishes to stay in darkness when we have God's glorious light available to us, especially, when we have the Holy Spirit to lead us into all truth.

## Evaluate

You have to evaluate everything that is taught to you. You need to ask the Holy Spirit for guidance and for discernment. He is the One who will lead you in the way of truth. He will tell you if something is wrong with what you are reading, with what you are seeing, or hearing. When you hear something that is preached, or when you see some demonstration on television or elsewhere that is supposed to be of God, but it is not, there will be a check inside of you that says, "Look again. Play that back again, and hear what was said. Check that in the Bible." Never ever discount that check inside you that says, "Wait a minute!" Just say, "Holy Spirit, speak to me. Show me Lord." He is your ultimate and true Guide. Listen to Him. If we do not correct this wrong that is in the Body of Christ right now, I do not think that it will be corrected before the Lord Jesus Christ returns. That is because I believe that He is coming soon.

## Correction

How can we bring correction to this error and fix the damage that has been done? Well, how did Jesus do it? He taught the truth. He brought light into the darkness of Israel when they desperately needed it; even though, they rejected it. He instructed His disciples, clarified the Scriptures to them, and showed them the wrongs that were being taught by the Pharisees, Sadducees and others. This is how He did it! We have to do the same.

## You Have a Father

In order to combat the orphan spirit syndrome, one of the first things that Jesus did was to make sure that His disciples understood that they had a father. He made certain that they knew that they did not have just any father, but that their Father was God. Furthermore, He made sure that they understood that He would never leave them nor forsake them.

"*Let not your heart be troubled; you believe in God, believe also in Me.*" (John 14:1) This is one of the most profound statements of Jesus in the Bible. First, Jesus tells us not to be afraid. This is because our number one enemy is fear. Fear is the tripper-upper, faith destroyer, hope killer, truth remover, doubt planter, and the death factor in Christendom. That is why Jesus' first statement here is, "*Do not be afraid.*"

29

## Believe in God

Jesus said, "*Believe in me.*" Well, you now believe in God, but do you believe in Jesus Christ? Many Pharisees, Sadducees, and other people also in those days did not believe in Jesus Christ as their Messiah. It is the same today. There are many who do not believe in Jesus. If you do not believe in Jesus, there is absolutely no salvation for you, there is no way for you to get to heaven. Jesus said to him, "*I am the way, the truth, and the life. No one comes to the Father except through Me.*" (John 14:6)

## One God

God's '*perfect love for us cancels out all fear*'. (I John 4:18) So your mind is clear. You believe in God and you believe in Jesus. This is important. It is also important to understand that, even though, they are two, yet are they one. Philip, Jesus' disciple, asked Him a certain question once, and Jesus answered him this way:

> "… Have I been with you so long, and yet you have not known Me, Philip? He who has seen Me has seen the Father; so how can you say, 'Show us the Father'? Do you not believe that I am in the Father, and the Father in Me? The words that I speak to you I do not speak on My own authority; but the Father who dwells in Me does the works. Believe Me that I am in the Father and the Father in Me, or else believe Me for the sake of the works themselves." (John 14:9-11)

There must be no doubt in your mind that God the Father, Jesus Christ and the Holy Spirit are one. If you are going to be freed from the orphan spirit's influence, force and lies, you will have to believe this truth. It is most important that you believe in the Trinity -- they are one.

Please understand that Jesus was speaking to Jews. If you study the Old Testament, you will find that the Jews did not relate to God as their Father, as much as they did to Abraham, Isaac and

Jacob. "*Therefore bear fruits worthy of repentance, and do not think to say to yourselves, 'We have Abraham as our father...'*" (Matthew 3:8-9) as well, "*He has helped His servant Israel, in remembrance of His mercy, as He spoke to our fathers, to Abraham and to his seed forever.*" (Luke 1:54-55)

## God is My Father

The Jews needed to understand that God was their Father, in order to truly see and believe that they were His children. This was a new concept that Jesus was teaching his followers. They needed to capture the truth of 'son-ship', so that as children of God they would be able to accept and receive His provisions for them. One of those provisions was His only begotten Son, Jesus Christ. You and I have to grab hold of this truth as well, that God is our Father. You are a child of God. When that sinks into your heart, it will change everything; not only when it enters your mind, but when it drops down into your heart. It has to become part of your being; a true reality deep within you. This truth that God is your Father has to be so real to you that it doesn't matter what happens, who said what, what experiences you had, or what you are experiencing now; nothing will be able to move you from this understanding and knowledge. When it has taken root in you, nothing can remove it from your heart.

In my many years of ministering to God's people, I have encountered numerous Christians who do not have a deep conviction that God is their Father. They think they believe that He is their Father, but it is only a shallow religious feeling that has no depth whatsoever. When any kind of wind or lies come blowing past, it knocks that shallow sense of 'God is my Father' out of their belief system. It destroys any trust they may have in God to provide for them or protect them... Satan then becomes bigger in their eyes. You must get this truth, "God is my Father" down past your throat. Many cannot do that because of the many lies that Satan has filled their hearts with, about themselves. They believe that they do not deserve to be God's child. After all, they

say, "Look at the life I have lived. God could not be my father."
He could save them through His Son, Jesus Christ, but to be their
father was far too much. They thought that they did not deserve
it. This idea is the biggest most catastrophic deception that Satan
creates in Christians with the orphan spirit syndrome.

Can we really prove that God is your Father? Is God truly
your Father just as He was and is Jesus' Father? And if He is Jesus'
Father, how can He be your Father? We are not simply speaking
of God as only, "God the Father" in the Trinity. The focus of our
discussion is to prove that this same Almighty God is your Father!
Jesus said, "*I will not leave you orphans; I will come to you.*" (John
14:18) If God says to you that He will not leave you as an orphan,
it means that He has provisions for you to have a father. He cannot
refer to you as an orphan and tell you that He will not leave you
as such; if He did not have provision to remedy your situation of
being an orphan.

Why did Jesus speak this truth to His disciples? In addition,
why does He also remind us of this now? Isn't it because He knew
the predicament that we would be in? Jesus knew that many would
feel like orphans and would feel rejected and lost, even though;
they are saved, even though they are on their way to Heaven. He
knew that many Christians would not understand the depth of
this son-ship or comprehend deep within them that God is their
Father. Looking 2,000 years ahead, Jesus saw that an orphan spirit
would be running wild in His Body, the Church. He wanted to
make sure that we would know that this was not His desire for us.
It is not where He desires for us to be. He said therefore, "*I will
not leave you as orphans.*" He also said,

> "*And I will pray the Father, and He will give
> you another Helper, that He may abide with you
> forever— the Spirit of truth, whom the world cannot
> receive, because it neither sees Him nor knows Him;
> but you know Him, for He dwells with you and will
> be in you.*" (John 14:16, 17)

He will live in you and be in you. The world cannot receive Him. Remember that! No wonder, they sometimes do not receive you, but He will be in you and with you. As a Christian, you must recognize that Jesus is in the Father or one with God the Father, and He lives in you by the Holy Spirit. *"A little while longer and the world will see Me no more, but you will see Me. Because I live, you will live also. At that day you will know that I am in My Father, and you in Me, and I in you."* (John 14:19, 20) Previously, He said, *"... I will come to you."* How did He come to you? as Holy Spirit and by the Holy Spirit! Yes, this is a great mystery and it is not easily explained.

The moment that you received Christ Jesus as your Lord and Saviour, the Holy Spirit came to live in your spirit. Furthermore, that is when Jesus came to you. However, not only Jesus came, but the Father also. Didn't Jesus say, *"My Father and I are one."*? (John 10:30) then again, *"Jesus answered and said to him, 'If anyone loves Me, he will keep My word; and My Father will love him, and We will come to him and make Our home with him.'"* (John 14:23)

Please remember and always keep this truth in your heart, God is your Father. You are His child — son or daughter. Moreover, He lives in you. Son-ship is yours and everything that comes with it. You must fully understand this truth to clearly see and comprehend the rest of our discussion in this book. I really want you to have no doubt in your heart that you are God's child, and that He is your Father.

As we proceed, you will now have a better picture of the revelations given by the Lord because you truly believe and know that God is your, Father. Paul called God, Father, *"To all who are in Rome, beloved of God, called to be saints: Grace to you and peace from God our Father and the Lord Jesus Christ."* (Romans 1:7) Then, again, *"For you did not receive the spirit of bondage again to fear, but you received the Spirit of adoption by whom we cry out, 'Abba, Father.'"* (Romans 8:15)

Dear God my Father, I thank you that you did not leave me as an orphan neither did you leave me in an orphanage, but you made me to be your child and to live in your home. You brought me out of darkness and placed me into your marvelous light. You saved me from hell and Satan and now I live in your Kingdom ⸗ free and empowered by your Holy Spirit to live holy and righteous all the days of my life on this earth. I ask that you will help me to always remember that you are my Father, that you love me more than anything else on this earth, that you desire the best for me and that your actions toward me are governed exclusively by your love. Help me to remember that you have forgiven all my sins, have erased them all and have forgotten them – they are no longer in your memory. Thank you that you will also forgive me at any time when I confess sins committed and you will cleanse me of all unrighteousness. I ask this is the name of Jesus Christ. Amen.

# 5

## LOSE THAT OLD LIFE!

*"For what profit is it to a man if he gains the*
*whole world, and loses his own soul? Or what*
*will a man give in exchange for his soul?"*
(Matthew 16:26)

Lose that old life…and everything associated with it. The Bible says, *"But those who lose their lives for me will find them. Whoever finds his life will lose it, and whoever loses his life for My sake will find it."* (Matthew 16:26) Have you lost your life? Do you plan to lose it? Would you like to lose it? Have you considered what would happen if you lose your life? What do you think would happen if you were to lose your life right now? What does that mean to you? If you were to say to someone that you have lost your life, what do you expect they would understand by that? My understanding is that if you lose your life, like Abraham leaving his old life with his family, it would mean losing everything that you own. You would lose mother, father, brother, sister, husband or wife, children, house, clothing, car, money, everything that was ever yours, and every inheritance that you would have inherited. When you lose your life, you really lose your life. It is all gone.

Jesus told His disciples that they would have to lose their lives if they were going to follow Him. "*Then He said to them all, 'If anyone desires to come after Me, let him deny himself, and take up his cross daily, and follow Me. For whoever desires to save his life will lose it, but whoever loses his life for My sake will save it. For what profit is it to a man if he gains the whole world, and is himself destroyed or lost?'*" (Luke 9:23–25) When Jesus told His disciples that they would need to deny themselves, leave off their old life, it meant they would take up a new life in Christ, including His name. Their previous life would be lost. They might have to change their legal name for the sake of protection. They might have to deny their family.

To deny one's self does not only include denying your own selfish desires, or giving up always having your own way and doing your own thing, but it requires also having to reject your past life and accept a new one in Jesus Christ.

> "*So that they should seek the Lord, in the hope that they might grope for Him and find Him, though He is not far from each one of us; for in Him we live and move and have our being, as also some of your own poets have said, 'For we are also His offspring.' Therefore, since we are the offspring of God, we ought not to think that the Divine Nature is like gold or silver or stone, something shaped by art and man's devising.*" (Acts 17:27–29)

In Him – Christ Jesus, you now live. In Him, you have your being. In Jesus Christ, you move, you live and exist. It is no longer you who live, you who have your being, you who exist. It is, "… *Christ in you the hope of glory.*" (Colossians 1:27)

When you were baptized in water, you were spiritually buried just as Jesus was after He was crucified. With that, you put away your old body, your old life, your sins, iniquities, and life style.

The 'old you died'. Since you lost your life, you must have died. If you died, then you must have been buried. If you were buried, stay buried! Because, if you stay buried, everything that was you and belonged to your past life, (character, attributes, way of thinking and acting, past lifestyle, all inheritances) will also remain dead and buried. *"Or do you not know that as many of us as were baptized into Christ Jesus were baptized into His death? Therefore we were buried with Him through baptism into death…"* (Romans 6:3, 4) Also, *"In Him you were also circumcised with the circumcision made without hands, by putting off the body of the sins of the flesh, by the circumcision of Christ, buried with Him in baptism…"* (Colossians 2:11, 12)

If you are born again, you are living a new life! You are alive in Him. You have a new life in Christ. Therefore, you are no longer the same. You are not the same person that you were before you 'died' to self. Since your 'new birth', your parents have lost you. They are no longer your parents. Please understand. The Bible says that you died. If you died and were buried, everybody would lose you. Since you died, the old you no longer exists; therefore, there is no inheritance for you either. Do not expect any! Who are they going to give it to? The old you does not exist! If they sent your earthly inheritance to your address, the mail man would not find you. If they shipped it collect, you wouldn't be there to sign for it. You would not be able to receive it, cash it in, or deposit it into a bank account. The old you does not exist in God's eyes. The law of God's grace abounds to the new person that you are; a new creation in Christ.

## A New Life

You have a new life. You are a different person. You have left off your old family and all that pertains to you from your past is dead, buried and gone. Therefore, as you are now alive in Christ, you must live that new life. Don't you agree? Well, is it true? Are you living a new life? To begin, though, you must answer this question: Did you receive a new life? Then, another question comes to mind. Were you given a new life? If you were given a new life, who is the one who gave it to you? You cannot receive something; if it was not given to you. You cannot be in possession of a thing when it is given to you, unless you accept it. Do you agree? So, have you fully accepted it? "... *Buried with Him in baptism, in which you also were raised with Him through faith in the working of God, who raised Him from the dead.*" (Colossians 2:12, 13)

I have a great Christian friend who is a powerful believer in every word God has put in the Bible. She stands on all emphatically. She can tell you how from her own experience, how from the young age of 13, her goal was to edit and write by water. She gave up on that idea as writers do not get paid till after the book is out. She then gave up a university career, gave up a government job, lost a business twice, lost her sister to heaven at the age of 30, and gave up on a marriage when she did not believe in divorce. In 2001, when the twin towers came down, she lost her international language school and $200,000 as well as lost her health. From the stress, she got extremely high blood pressure and almost died many times over. She was at death's door one time when she rose up powerfully in faith and declared to God "This is not the end of me, we have work to do." Within a year, God had her editing and writing by water. She had been taking 18 pills a day to stay alive and did not think she could ever teach or write again.

Yet, a few years later, God had her go on two of her own funded mission trips to India where she preached the Gospel daily in churches and to pastors and prayed through slum areas and orphanages. In 2016, she opened a Christian Publishing House in India. When Hindu extremists attacked and burned the place to the ground, she lost 150,000 of God's books in the Hyderabad fire. She then decided to really let all fall as dead seeds to the ground as the Word says '*Except a seed fall to the ground, it cannot bring forth new life.*" Did she lose all? Yes, many things many times over. However, here is her clincher... She knows and states that God just does not heal us or just restore us to how we were before (like taking us back as we were before)...NO! He brings us back to the top at a much higher level where we never were before. He sets us upon a rock and exalts us spiritually, mentally and physically much higher and better than we could have ever made ourselves. In her spiritual faith walk, she lost all, but she GAVE ALL BACK TO GOD TO DO WITH IT AS HE HAD ALWAYS PLANNED TO DO. She could then see WHAT GREATER WAY HE HAD FOR HER TO GO.... Now in 2017, she is waiting on a mighty move of God that will totally lift her up to a higher plane where she has never been before. God's perfect will to be carried out! THAT IS ALL GOD.

IMAGINE... why is it a big deal for God to ask His people to 'lose their lives for Him'? How much did He lose of all for us?

Then again, *"...just as Christ was raised from the dead by the glory of the Father, even so we also should walk in newness of life."* (Romans 6:3, 4) Jesus Christ who was resurrected from the dead has a new life *"sitting at the right hand of the Father judging both the quick and the dead."* (II Timothy 4:1) He is no longer walking around on this earth in the flesh. He is not tied down to a fleshy body anymore that kept Him tied to one place and to one location constantly. Now, by His Holy Spirit, He can live in you, and me, and anyone else who will receive Him. Isn't it wonderful that you yourself weren't left in the grave to decay? Aren't you thankful that God didn't leave you to corrupt in the earth? He raised you up! *"For if we have been united together in the likeness of His death, certainly we also shall be in the likeness of His resurrection."* (Romans 6:5) He resurrected you just like He resurrected His Son, Jesus Christ. Isn't that awesome? Yes, my friend, God is awesome and He does awesome things. Don't you love Him? I do.

You were united with Jesus our Saviour in death, and certainly you were joined with Him in His resurrection. Therefore, you have received life in Him and you are definitely living a new life. It has absolutely nothing to do with the old one you used to have! Can you see this now? Do you understand what Paul is saying in the above verse of scriptures? *"And you, being dead in your trespasses*

*and the uncircumcision of your flesh, He has made alive together with*
*Him, having forgiven you all trespasses."* (Colossians 2:13)

God forgave you all of your sins. He does not remember them
anymore. He made you alive *together* with Jesus, not apart from
Him. Forget your past sins. Do not remember them. Do not think
or dwell on them. No longer do you have to keep asking God for
forgiveness for them. They are gone, they are erased! He does not
remember them anymore. This is the greatest gift of all time and
it is for you. May I make a suggestion? Do not bother God with
your past sins. Talk to Him about your present life. Discuss your
future with Him. Ask Him what His desires are for you. Tell Him
what is in your heart, what you want to do, and what you would
like for Him to do for you. Share with Him your dreams and
aspirations. He may give you a new vision for your life. Perhaps,
He will lay out a map for you to follow. The Lord may give you a
plan of action. He will do all this for you if you will only ask Him.
Trust Him! Have you made the connection between your life and
Christ's, yet? This is what Jesus said, *"Because I live, you will live*
*also."* (John 14:9) You must acknowledge that you are now living
by His life. Remember, you live in Him and through Him now.

## One with Him

Well, now your life is in Christ Jesus, do you fully understand
that your old life is passed away and buried? That you have no more
inheritance to obtain from your past life? And that your parents,
spiritually speaking, are no longer legally your parents? In other
words, you and Christ have become one. You are in Him and He
is in you. That's a mystery. Since your new life is in Christ Jesus
and you are one with Him, His Father is your Father! *"At that*
*day you will know that I am in My Father, and you in Me, and I in*
*you."* (John 14:20)

Jesus' last prayer in the Garden of Gethsemane was a prayer
about us — about people that had not even been born yet. He had
no idea what we would even look like. He prayed:

*"That they all may be one, as You, Father, are in Me, and I in You; that they also may be one in Us, that the world may believe that You sent Me. And the glory which You gave Me I have given them, that they may be one just as we are one: I in them, and You in Me; that they may be made perfect in one, and that the world may know that You have sent Me, and have loved them as You have loved Me. And I have declared to them Your name, and will declare it, that the love with which You loved Me may be in them, and I in them."* (John 17:21-23, 26)

As well, *"For you are all sons of God through faith in Christ Jesus. For as many of you as were baptized into Christ have put on Christ. There is neither Jew nor Greek, there is neither slave nor free, there is neither male nor female; for you are all one in Christ Jesus."* (Galatians 3:26–28)

Why don't you take this moment right now to just thank the Lord for what He has done for you? Thank Him for thinking about you before you were born. Thank him for giving you a new life. Thank Him for salvation. Thank Him for freeing you into His Kingdom and preparing you for Heaven. Thank Him for eternity. Thank Him for **everything**!

Dear Father God, thank You that my new life is in Christ Jesus my Lord and my Saviour. Thank You that it is He who lives in and through me and gives me strength. It is by Your Holy Spirit that You keep me and work out Your own plan and purpose for my life. I am assured that each day I am led by You and You will never fail me. I am alive and well and You cause everything to work together for my good. I give You thanks in the name of Jesus Christ my Lord and my Saviour. Amen.

# 6

## GENERATIONAL CURSE

*"...for I, the Lord your God, am a jealous
God, visiting the iniquity of the fathers
upon the children to the third and fourth
generations."*
(Exodus 20:5)

The term 'generational curse' comes from the Book of Exodus Chapter 20. In those days, Israelites had turned from God to serve idols, which angered the Lord. He then pronounced punishments on the descendants of those idol worshippers in Israel, up to the third and fourth generation of children. This is why it is called, 'a generational curse'.

Paul and Barnabas, much later, in the New Testament had a confrontation with the other Apostles that almost exploded into something very serious. The entire young Church could have split up into many tiny pieces. The highly contested matter was in regard to social issues of the Old Testament versus the New Testament. Should they practise this or should they practise the other? Must the Gentiles do the same things as the Jews? Didn't they worship the same God? Therefore, what was good for the Jews was good for the Gentiles, wasn't it? The fact of the matter is that they were no longer under the Mosaic Law. There were certain requirements then, just as there are today, but they had to be defined. Clarity was needed. Thus, many discussions arose both inside and outside the Church, at home, and out on the mission field.

One of the arguments was about circumcision. Shouldn't the Gentile Christians be circumcised as Jewish Christians were?

> *"And certain men came down from Judea and taught the brethren, 'Unless you are circumcised according to the custom of Moses, you cannot be saved.' Therefore, when Paul and Barnabas had no small dissension and dispute with them, they determined that Paul and Barnabas and certain others of them should go up to Jerusalem, to the apostles and elders, about this question."* (Acts 15:1, 2)

Jerusalem was the Church headquarters. This was where matters of the Body of Christ were deliberated and discussed. So Paul and Barnabas went to meet them. *"But some of the sect of the Pharisees who believed rose up, saying, "It is necessary to circumcise them, and to command them to keep the Law of Moses."* (Acts 15:5) The 'wise guys' said, that they had to be circumcised. They were the elite when it came to the Law. They knew it inside and out, forwards and backwards so they insisted that the Gentiles be circumcised.

> *"Now the apostles and elders came together to consider the matter. And when there had been much dispute, Peter rose up and said to them: "Men and brethren, you know that a good while ago God chose among us, that by my mouth the Gentiles should hear the word of the Gospel and believe. So God, who knows the heart, acknowledged them by giving them the Holy Spirit, just as He did to us, and made*

> *no distinction between us and them, purifying their*
> *hearts by faith. Now therefore, why do you test God*
> *by putting a yoke on the neck of the disciples which*
> *neither our fathers nor we were able to bear? But*
> *we believe that through the grace of the Lord Jesus*
> *Christ we shall be saved in the same manner as they."*
> (Acts 15:6 – 11)

As you can see, this was not just a simple, 'yes' or 'no' affair. They deliberated for hours and argued the case for a lengthy period of time. They had to be sure about it before presenting it to the Body of Christ. They could not just simply tell the children of God to do something that was not warranted, or demanded of God.

Peter pointed out a number of things here that are important to our own discussion. God gave the Holy Spirit to the Jews and Gentile Christians alike. He did not make a division or difference between them. They all received salvation through faith and God's grace. Then, though, he said something that is so important, "… *why do you test God by putting a yoke on the neck of the disciples which neither our fathers nor we were able to bear?*" (Acts 15:10) The Jews of old could not bear the yoke or carry the burden of the Law, yet the Pharisees who had become Christians wanted the Gentiles to have this yoke.

> *"Then all the multitude kept silent and listened to*
> *Barnabas and Paul declaring how many miracles*
> *and wonders God had worked through them among*
> *the Gentiles. And after they had become silent, James*
> *answered, saying, 'Men and brethren, listen to me:*
> *Simon has declared how God at the first visited the*
> *Gentiles to take out of them a people for His name.*
> *And with this the words of the prophets agree, just*
> *as it is written: 'After this I will return and will*
> *rebuild the tabernacle of David, which has fallen*
> *down; I will rebuild its ruins, and I will set it up;*
> *so that the rest of mankind may seek the Lord, even*

*all the Gentiles who are called by My name, says
the Lord who does all these things.' Known to God
from eternity are all His works … For Moses has
had throughout many generations those who preach
him in every city, being read in the synagogues every
Sabbath."* (Acts 15:12-21)

## The Jerusalem Decree

Then it pleased the apostles and elders, with the whole church,
to send chosen men of their own company to Antioch with Paul and
Barnabas, *namely,* Judas who was also named Barsabas, and Silas,
leading men among the brethren. They wrote this letter, *by them:*

*The apostles, the elders, and the brethren,*

*To the brethren who are of the Gentiles in Antioch,
Syria, and Cilicia:*

*"Greetings,*

*Since we have heard that some who went out from us
have troubled you with words, unsettling your souls,
saying, 'You must be circumcised and keep the Law'
—to whom we gave no such commandment— it
seemed good to us, being assembled with one accord,
to send chosen men to you with our beloved Barnabas
and Paul, men who have risked their lives for the
name of our Lord Jesus Christ. We have therefore
sent Judas and Silas, who will also report the same
things by word of mouth. For it seemed good to the
Holy Spirit, and to us, to lay upon you no greater
burden than these necessary things: that you abstain
from things offered to idols, from blood, from things
strangled, and from sexual immorality. If you keep
yourselves from these, you will do well. Farewell."*
(Acts 15:12-29)

Like the apostles of old, we must also be diligent and, with the help of the Holy Spirit, ponder, deliberate, and properly interpret the Word of God for ourselves before presenting the conclusion to God's people. This is no light matter. This is crucial for the good of all who read, watch or listen. We owe them that much, but more than that, we are accountable to the Lord for whatever we teach and preach.

## Generational Curse

A 'generational curse' is a widely misunderstood subject. Therefore, many Christians are in bondage because of it. Misconstrued knowledge which has not been thoroughly examined is detrimental to anyone, who chooses to accept it as it is. It is terribly sad that this is exactly what has happened to a great number of Christians today. Almost everyone, who talks about 'generational curses', discusses a very prominent and respected author, teacher and preacher's teachings on the subject. Here is what he wrote -- "With a shock, you begin to wonder if the cause of your problems could be the same: *a curse going back to preceding generations.*" Then again, "A curse could also be likened to a long, evil arm stretched out from the past. It rests upon you with a dark oppressive force that inhibits…" (Derek Prince, "Blessing or Curse: You Can Choose")

In his writings, Derek Prince attempts to prove that Christians are sometimes under a curse from 'preceding generations' or that they are under this 'long, evil arm stretched out from the past'. Many refer to these terms under the one term, 'generational curse'. Look closely to what was written and consider whether what he says is true according to the Bible. Is it true? Can a Christian be under a "long, evil arm stretched out from the past" or can they be under "a curse going back to the preceding generations"? What is Derek Prince saying? What is he referring to in these quotes? Is his reference correct? Should he or we refer to 'generational curses', in the context of 'born again believers'?

Derek Prince wrote: "On a ministry journey in Southeast Asia, I met an intelligent, well-educated female judge, who was descended from royalty. She knew Jesus personally as her Saviour and was not conscious of any unconfessed sin in her life. Yet, she told me that she was not truly satisfied. Her successful career and her high social position had not brought her personal fulfillment. As I talked with her, I discovered that she was descended from many generations of idol worshipers. I explained to her that, according to Exodus 20:3–5, God had pronounced a curse on idol worshipers down to the third and fourth generations. Then, I showed her how to receive release from this curse through Jesus her Saviour." (His book, "Blessing or Curse: You Can Choose")

A number of things can be noted in this conversation between Derek Prince and this woman. First of all, she was of royal birth, and had the best education; then she was a judge. Obviously, she was very successful. She must have lacked for nothing materially. She had a high position in society, and I am sure that she must have been highly respected in her community. Last, but, of course, not least, she had Jesus as her personal Saviour – she was born again.

However, with all of this going for her, she did not have, 'personal fulfilment'. So we, therefore, must assume that she was under a curse from her past. Are you kidding me? What does personal fulfilment have to do with curses from one's past? If she had Jesus Christ as her Lord and Saviour, but did not personally feel fulfilled; it is obvious that she was looking in the wrong place for her fulfilment. However, let's play along to try to understand the subject a bit better. Let us go along with this assumption that she was under 'a curse' from the past, which made her feel personally unfulfilled. If she was born again; how could she be under a curse from her past generations of relatives who were idol worshipers?

This is the whole point of the issue, isn't it? Can we be under a 'generational curse' if we are born again?

Derek Prince demonstrated to this female judge that she was under a curse from her forefathers according to Exodus 20:3–5. He is not the only teacher who refers to these verses of scripture in relation to 'generational curses'; many others do as well. Let us see what Exodus 20:3-5 really says:

> *"And God spoke all these words, saying: 'I am the Lord your God, who brought you out of the land of Egypt, out of the house of bondage. You shall have no other gods before Me. You shall not make for yourself a carved image—any likeness of anything that is in heaven above, or that is in the earth beneath, or that is in the water under the earth; you shall not bow down to them nor serve them. For I, the Lord your God, am a jealous God, **visiting the iniquity of the fathers upon the children to the third and fourth generations of those who hate Me**, but showing mercy to thousands, to those who love Me and keep My commandments.'"* (Exodus 20:1–5) (Highlight is mine)

I have added verses one and two so that we may be able to see who God was speaking to and why.

At this time in history, when the Lord spoke to Moses, many of the Israelites had turned their backs on God and were worshipping idols. God was angry with them so pronounced a curse on them. He told them that their children would be punished for their idolatry up to the third and fourth generation. I want to stress the point here again, as I have elsewhere, that when the Lord said, *'visiting the iniquity of the fathers upon the children',* He was not saying that He **would** *put* the iniquity of the fathers upon the children. Yet, some Christian scholars interpret this portion of scripture this way. It is wrong! God will not *put* sin on anyone nor will He tempt anyone. Iniquity is simply the continuous practice of sin -- constant, habitual sinning.

Therefore, God is speaking about punishing the children for the sins of their forefathers, up until the third and fourth generations. *"Let no one say when he is tempted, 'I am tempted by God;' for God cannot be tempted by evil, nor does He Himself tempt anyone."* (James 1:13) He is not saying that He *will put or pass on* the sin or sinful practices of the forefathers upon the children. The immediate question that must follow is this: Did this pronounced curse pass from the Old Testament into the New Testament? If it did, then we **do have a major problem**. When we have the correct answer to this question, we will be on our way, in the right direction.

Now, this raises many questions. Was this curse pronounced by God upon the Israelites? (Exodus 20:3–5) What did God do about this curse? Did He do anything about it? Or did He just allow it to continue to occur upon Israel? How long does this pronouncement go on for -- forever? Or is there an end? Are Christians included in this curse? Does it include born again believers? Did God ever deal with it? To begin with, it was a curse pronounced upon Israel, but not on all the Israelites. It was only upon those who turned from worshipping God to 'worship idols'. If it was a curse pronounced upon Israel, we must first look at it from the standpoint of God and Israel. Check this out, *"The word of the Lord came to me again, saying, 'What do you mean when you use this proverb concerning the land of Israel, saying: The fathers have eaten sour grapes, and the children's teeth are set on edge'? 'As I live,' says the Lord God, 'you shall no longer use this proverb in Israel."* (Ezekiel 18:1-3) What is the Lord talking about? What is He referring to?

Well, this was a common proverb used at this time in Israel. It was frequently used to describe punishment, especially, punishment that had to do with exactly what was pronounced in Exodus. This proverb simply meant that the fathers had sinned, and the children would pay the price. God had had enough of it! So, suddenly,

He commanded Ezekiel to demand of the Israelites that none of them were to use this word ever again. "*You shall no longer use this proverb.*" No longer, means **no longer**. Since that is the case, God must have meant He would do something about the source of this proverb. "*Behold, all souls are Mine; the soul of the father as well as the soul of the son is Mine; the soul who sins shall die.*" (Ezekiel 18:4) Obviously, this meant that the one who sinned would pay for his sins. The father's children would no longer be punished for his sins.

Ezekiel 18:19 not only speaks to this, but also prophesies from the past what would come in the new time of our Lord Jesus Christ's death:

> "*Yet you say, 'Why should the son not bear the guilt of the father?' Because the son has done what is lawful and right, and has kept all My statutes and observed them, he shall surely live. The soul who sins shall die. The son shall not bear the guilt of the father, nor the father bear the guilt of the son. The righteousness of the righteous shall be upon himself, and the wickedness of the wicked shall be upon himself.*" (Ezekiel 18:19)

It cannot be any clearer for Christians. God dealt with the curse that He had pronounced upon Israel. Here in Ezekiel, He totally erased it. See for yourself. Look at the above verse again. "*Why should the son not bear the guilt of the father? ... The son shall **not** bear the guilt of the father, nor should the father bear the guilt of the son.*" Could it be more obvious? God solved this problem of 'generational curses', right in the Old Testament. It did not come over to the New Testament. It was spoken, fulfilled and removed in the Old Testament. In the Gospel of John, we later read and understand, "*A new commandment I give to you, that you love one another; as I have loved you, that you also love one another. By this all will know that you are My disciples, if you have love for one another.*" (John 13:34-35) Your new covenant in Christ has one law. Remember, the Old Testament is the old covenant under Moses.

The New Testament was instituted, fulfilled, made, and governed in and by Jesus Christ our Lord and Saviour.

I do not believe that Jewish people ever talk about having a generational curse upon their lives today. Why do we Christians do so? Your new life in Christ has nothing to do with the old covenant and its laws. As a born again believer, when you received Jesus Christ as your Lord and your Saviour, you received a new life. This new life has no connection to the old one. You did not inherit generational curses or any other kind of curses when you began your new life in Christ Jesus.

Then you raise the question: Can a Christian be under a curse? Yes! "But you just said…" That is all about generational curses, or curses passed on from father to son to son. However, in this new life as a Christian, a believer can come under a curse by his own doing. A curse can come upon him by his own words spoken over his life. Do you realise how powerful your words are? Do you know that there are so many born again believers under a curse right now because of something they themselves have spoken into their own life? Most of it, they have called upon themselves. There is power in what you say, and many times people call into or over their own lives the influence, death and destruction of Satan. Curses come from the result of events in peoples' own lives. It is also a result of their own words. *"Death and life are in the power of the tongue, and those who love it will eat its fruit."* (Proverbs 18:21) And again,

> *"And the tongue is a fire, a world of iniquity. The tongue is so set among our members that it defiles the whole body, and sets on fire the course of nature; and it is set on fire by hell… with it we bless our God and Father, and with it we curse men, who have been made in the similitude of God. Out of the same mouth proceed blessing and cursing."* (James 3:6, 9-10)

A friend of mine recently told me an amazing story. I will leave it as she told me:

In the last month, I had an experience that helped me recognize the power of our words even more clearly. I went to a dentist for a not very complicated procedure -- for a filling, but 3 days later my tooth was still very sore and I was in pain. I then went to a prayer meeting, where I heard the testimony of a woman and how she had received God's healing several times in her life. I was so impressed by her testimony, I asked her to pray for me. I really did not want any complications with my tooth and definitely I did not want a root canal.

I embraced the idea that I would receive healing. For the next 2 weeks, I thus faithfully prayed and believed, and renounced every thought that led in a different direction. Even though I still had pain, it became better and better... surely it did not get worse. This gave me the assurance that I was on the right track and that full restoration was imminent.

In two weeks, I received a call from that same lady who asked me how I was doing. She even offered to pay for a dentist visit, if I still needed one. I told her that I was still in pain, but I felt better and better every day. I trusted that I would not need a root canal. She said her husband was a dentist, so she knew that if the pain was so persistent, I probably had a tooth infection or gum infection. She advised me to get the dentist to give me an antibiotic. It sounded reasonable to me, so I agreed to see my dentist.

That night, for the first time after the filling, I could not sleep because of the pain. The next day was quite busy, so I did not have time to visit the dentist. Instead, I phoned him to ask for a prescription for an antibiotic. Of course, he did not agree to give it to me without seeing me, so I tried to convince him that I really needed it, as I had an infection. I told him I had had pain during the night so I was concerned it might become worse. He still refused so I ended up going to see him the next day. I again told him how I had pain and infection, which had got worse. He x-rayed my tooth; saying that I did not have an infection so did not need antibiotics. He said that using a stronger mouthwash would be enough.

To my surprise, the next day, I woke up with pain in another tooth that I had had a root canal and crown on more than 10 years ago. I had never had problems with it before. For the next couple of days, the pain progressed, and it became sensitive to cold and hot, and to touch. Finally, that side of my mouth was swollen with inflammation. I imagined that I needed to go back to the dentist to explain to him again that I now had an infection -- this time on a different tooth.

Suddenly, it hit me. I finally had the infection that I had been declaring for the last couple of days. I believed I had it. I had proclaimed it. I acted on it and got it!!! Not okay! Therefore, for the first 2 weeks, I had held onto my vision of healing; even when I had not received it right away. There had been an improvement day after day. However, after that, I had heard the word 'infection', which had made its way into my spirit. I had accepted it for me instead of standing on my healing. I watered it with my meditation and proclamation -- the fruit of it was that the real infection came. Two choices confronted me -- to go to a dentist again, or to reverse the spiritual process, which had led me to the place of physical infection.

Isaiah 54:17 says: "*No weapon formed against thee shall prosper; and every tongue that shall rise against thee in judgment thou shalt condemn. This is the heritage of the servants of the Lord, and their righteousness is of Me,' saith the Lord.*" So 'a tongue' (spoken words) had been raised against me so against the healing that I believed in, I now had to condemn. The definition of condemn is: "to express complete disapproval of, typically in public; to censure; to express an unfavorable or adverse judgment on; to indicate strong disapproval of; to judge or pronounce to be unfit for use or service".

When I had heard the word 'infection', I did not 'express or indicate complete and strong disapproval' of it nor 'express an unfavorable and adverse judgment on them'. I actually agreed with the words! I did not pronounce them 'unfit for use'. I actually pronounced it helpful and smart! So in order to reverse the process, in my spirit, I had to go back to the time when I had heard and accepted 'infection' for the first time. I then had to do what I had failed to do then. I condemned it and 'expressed complete and strong disapproval of it. I pronounced the words unfit for my use. I thus broke any power that those words had on me. In four hours every sign of infection was gone!

Therefore, I must reiterate what you say -- either brings blessing into your life, or brings curses. You choose each and every day what you receive at the end of the day, and in your future. You are constantly calling it in. So, what are you calling in? Derek Prince again wrote, "Often such people say something like, 'The same thing always happened to my father: I feel as if I'm reliving his frustrations...'" Those people were under a curse because they had called it into their lives themselves. How? Every time they said things like, "The same thing always happened to my father. I'm reliving his frustrations." This person pronounced a curse on his own life when he declared he was *reliving his father's frustrations*.

You will often hear people say, "This time of year, I always get a cold." The next thing that happens is that they are sick with a cold. They specified the time and also specified that it be continuously -- always theirs. They got what they had spoken about. Sometimes again, you will hear someone say, "My mother had arthritis and I know I am going to have it too." Or someone else may say, "My father died from diabetes and I know I will too." Others may say it like this, "Oh, I have to be so careful because my mother had brittle bones." Two things happen: that person is constantly living in fear of having brittle bones, and as long as that goes on, there is no faith from that person to trust God for safety and security from that disease.

Life and death sit on your tongue and whenever you decide to spew something out, one of them will jump out. You can choose which one. There is a saying too, which you should fully understand. "You can either live dying or die living." It is your choice alone how you live -- blessed or cursed. If you are still not convinced, here is what Jesus told His disciples. "*So Jesus answered and said to them, 'Have faith in God. For assuredly, I say to you, whoever says to this mountain, 'Be removed and be cast into the sea,' and does not doubt in his heart, but believes that those things he says will be done, he will have whatever he says.'*" (Mark 11:22-23) What did Jesus tell His disciples would happen when they speak and believe? "*He will have whatever he says.*"

If you pronounce such curses and judgements on your life; you are putting curses on yourself and into your life. Listen, it is not me who says this. Jesus said it! The Bible says it. The tongue boasts or speaks many things. It can set a whole nation on fire. You know how that is. Imagine the internet and a similar means of communication today. If someone were to Tweet something right now, in a matter of minutes, millions would know about it. Talk about setting the forest on fire! James says that the tongue is set on fire of hell, but it doesn't have to be that way. If you renew your mind by filling your heart and mind with God's Word; your tongue will speak the right things and you will have the right results. Proverbs 13:2 says, "*A man shall eat well by the fruit of his mouth…*"

I encourage you; therefore, put your faith in God. Stop believing that you have a generational curse. Renounce the known negative evil words that you have spoken over your life. Ask the Lord for forgiveness for speaking them, and ask Him to erase them from your life. Then begin to speak the Word of God into your life as it is "*sharper than a two edged sword*". (Hebrews 4:12) It will change your life and cause God's blessing to manifest in it. Furthermore, Psalm 3:8 says, "*Salvation belongs to the Lord. Your blessing is upon Your people.*"

Dear God my Father, I declare that I am not cursed and I have no generational curses in or upon my life. You have redeemed me from every curse. Your blessing is upon my life. I am greatly blessed and highly favoured. My inheritance is from you. I have inherited from you life in abundance, grace in all sufficiency, love and joy, peace that is beyond all understanding, power in the name of Jesus Christ, the covering of the blood of Jesus Christ, and all spiritual blessings in heavenly places. I never lose! I always WIN. I declare it in Jesus' name. Amen.

# 7

## WHO IS YOUR ENEMY?

*"...principalities, powers, the rulers of
the darkness of this age,spiritual hosts of
wickedness in the heavenly places'*
(Ephesians 6:12)

As long as you believe that you are under a curse, you will never deal with the real 'strongman'-- the devil, who is stealing your happiness, as well as destroying, hindering, and putting death upon your life. Your enemy is not 'generational curses'. These curses are not what is tormenting your life and bringing destruction on you. Your enemy is subtle, and is happy to let you continue to believe that you are under a generational curse. If you cannot recognize the exact demon that is operating in your life; you will not be able to bind him and destroy his works. Therefore, he will be happy to hide behind any lies and continue to create and cause you havoc.

If we take a close look at the New Testament, we find that Jesus was always specific in dealing with what and whom He encountered. You will find that He always confronted the specific demon operating in the life of the captive. He would proceed to cast out that demon to liberate the enslaved person. In your life, you have to do the same. You have to find the specific demon spirit operating in your life -- bind it, break its powers and cast it into the Abyss to set yourself free from it.

## Anger Destroys

Who is the enemy? Can you define your enemy more clearly? Who is it that is possibly operating in your life right now and bringing harm to you? These are still questions that need to be answered. Your life's battle is not against people. It is against an unseen force called evil spirits. We read in Ephesians: *"For we do not wrestle against flesh and blood, but against principalities, against powers, against the rulers of the darkness of this age, against spiritual hosts of wickedness in the heavenly places."* (Ephesians 6:12) You are not fighting people -- flesh and blood. People do not bring damnation, destruction, and death into your life, Satan does. When you are angry at other people, you will more than likely attack them with your words, with your attitude, and even in your prayers. However, they are not your enemy! Your enemy is the devil.

Too many times, instead of confronting Satan and his host of evil spirits, people put their effort, time and strength into remaining unhappy and being angry with other people. Some people get so angry with others that they remain with unforgiveness and a consuming bitterness in their hearts for years. You have a right to be angry if you were hurt by someone; however, you shouldn't stay angry. When you get angry with others who have hurt you; you must not remain angry with them for the rest of your life! Listen, if you are angry with someone for some reason, stop now! You are only hurting yourself. If you have not forgiven them for hurting you -- it does not matter what it was about; you are only hurting yourself. You cannot achieve your victory in life while being consumed with anger. You must only forgive them, and leave them in the hands of God. Then, move on. If not, you are going to be tied to that past and remain there for the rest of your life. Often people put their focus on the wrong thing, in the wrong direction when it comes to their daily matters of life, not wanting to admit that it is evil spirits working in people that have attacked them not the people themselves.

In the meantime, the other folks that you got angry at are moving on with their lives while you continue to hurt. In this way, you have left an open door of unforgiveness in your life for the devil, and he will continue to walk in and work damnation there. You have no choice but to forgive everyone who has hurt you, pray for them, and leave them in the hands of the Lord. You will be amazed at what you will see the Lord can accomplish in those people's lives. You only help yourself when you forgive. I have written at length on forgiveness in my book, 'What You Weren't Told about Righteousness'. I encourage you to read it as it will tremendously bless you.

The devil may use people to bring harm to you, but they are absolutely not your enemy.

Realize today that those people that Satan has used to hurt you are victims of a cunning devil. Their lives have been infiltrated, trespassed upon by Satan so they are under his control to some degree, at least in the situation in which they were used to cause hurt to you. He cannot use them unless he has them in his grip. They have, therefore, become his victims. They themselves need our prayers for liberation from the enemy. So then, you need to pray for them rather than be angry at them. Don't you agree?

Do you see now, how you can leave the door open for Satan to enter in and cause havoc in your life? When you haven't forgiven someone because they hurt you, your sins are not forgiven by God. This brings a separation from God, which Satan takes advantage of. You leave an open door for him to operate in your life. Just one door is usually all he needs. Quit being angry with those who have hurt you, forgive them, and you will immediately shut this door. Always pray the Lord's Prayer over all your situations:

*"Our Father in heaven, Hallowed be Your
name. Your kingdom come. Your will be done
On earth as it is in heaven. Give us this day
our daily bread. And forgive us our debts, As
we forgive our debtors. And do not lead us into
temptation, But deliver us from the evil one.
For Yours is the kingdom and the power and the
glory forever. Amen."* (Matthew 6:9-13)

Again, we can read, *"For if you forgive men their trespasses, your
heavenly Father will also forgive you. But if you do not forgive men their
trespasses, neither will your Father forgive your trespasses."* (Matthew
6:8-15) Can you imagine how it will be if your sins are just piling
up because they are not forgiven by God? Now, that is only one
door. There are many others that we need to find and close.

We can read in the Gospel of Mark that even Jesus got angry
with the Jewish people who had made the temple into a market
place, selling birds and other things for sacrifices and offerings.

*"So they came to Jerusalem. Then Jesus went into
the temple and began to drive out those who bought
and sold in the temple, and overturned the tables of
the money changers and the seats of those who sold
doves. And He would not allow anyone to carry
wares through the temple. Then He taught, saying
to them, "Is it not written, 'My house shall be called
a house of prayer for all nations'? But you have made
it a 'den of thieves.'"* (Mark 11:15-17)

Yet, what did Jesus pray at the end of His life about all, *"Forgive
them for they know not what they do."* (Luke 23:34) This is what
we must do as well.

## The Enemy

When you look at the army of any country, you will find that
it is set up in various ranks, from the highest to the lowest. The

generals give the orders and the lower ranking soldiers carry out the commands. It is the same with Satan's army that he has set up on the earth. They are set up in various ranks such as we see here in Ephesians 6:12 'principalities, powers, the rulers of the darkness of this age, spiritual hosts of wickedness in the heavenly places'. Principalities are the highest ranking evil spirits. They govern the rest. How can we prove that?

Daniel was praying for twenty one days. Suddenly one day, the angel of God appeared and told him that his prayers had been answered on the very first day that he had begun to pray. However, as this angel traveled towards Daniel to bring the answer to him, he was blocked and hindered from coming to Daniel. He couldn't come to the man of God so he had to call upon the Lord for help. When he did, the Lord sent the Archangel Michael to help him.

> "In those days I, Daniel, was mourning three full weeks. I ate no pleasant food, no meat or wine came into my mouth, nor did I anoint myself at all, till three whole weeks were fulfilled.
>
> Now on the twenty-fourth day of the first month..., I lifted my eyes and looked, and behold, a certain man clothed in linen, whose waist was girded with gold of Uphaz! His body was like beryl, his face like the appearance of lightning, his eyes like torches of fire, his arms and feet like burnished bronze in color, and the sound of his words like the voice of a multitude. Suddenly, a hand touched me, which made me tremble on my knees and on the palms of my hands. And he said to me, 'O Daniel, man greatly beloved, understand the words that I speak to you, and stand upright, for I have now been sent to you.' While he was speaking this word to me, I stood trembling. Then he said to me, 'Do not fear, Daniel, for from the first day that you set your heart to understand, and to humble yourself before your God, your words were

*heard; and I have come because of your words. But* the **Prince of the kingdom of Persia withstood me twenty-one days;** *and behold, Michael, one of the chief princes, came to help me, for I had been left alone there with the kings of Persia. Now I have come to make you understand what will happen to your people in the latter days, for the vision refers to many days yet to come.'"* (Daniel 10:2-6; 10-14)

Who was this '*Prince of the Kingdom of Persia'* who withstood him? This was not a human being. He definitely was not the King of Persia nor was he one of the princes of Persia. The Angel of God is not human so cannot be stopped by humans. Therefore, we must understand that it was a spiritual being and as such, an enemy of God and His angels. This 'Prince of Persia' could only be an evil spirit who was the highest ranking demon, controlling Persia. He had a title 'Prince' of the Kingdom of Persia. He, therefore, had dominion over a territory or principality, which was Persia.

Thus, since it was an evil spirit of hell, the prince over a territory that opposed the angel of God, where and how was he opposing him? Was it on the earth, or in the heavens? Where did this battle take place? "*And you He made alive, who were dead in trespasses and sins, in which you once walked according to the course of this world, according to* **the prince of the power of the air**, *the spirit who now works in the sons of disobedience*" (Ephesians 2:1, 2) Where is this 'prince', the 'spirit' who works in the sons of disobedience? He is in the air, or in the heavenly areas. He is not directly here on the earth. He is above us in the heavens. Now, we know who we are really fighting and where they are according to Ephesians 2:1-2; 6:12. Therefore, our battle is against the forces of Satan which are set up in the air or in the heavenly places and contend for our lives. It is not against people.

## Who is Hindering Me?

So what is it that is hindering your life? What is keeping you back from your full potential? Why do you struggle with what seems to be the same or similar sins of your forefathers? Why is it that your life is not going the way you planned or expected it to be? What is the hindrance? Satan comes at you to steal from you, kill you, and to totally destroy everything that you have worked for or accomplished. "*The thief does not come except to steal, and to kill, and to destroy...*" (John 10:10)

Who is this thief? It is no other than the devil himself, whom Jesus is speaking about. It is Satan himself and his hosts of evil spirits. They are the ones who are hindering you, tripping you up, and disrupting your progress. He wants to defeat you even before you begin to make inroads in any area of your life. He doesn't want you to succeed! Why? When you succeed who do you give the glory to? Who is glorified every time something good happens in your life? Who do you give the praises to when wonderful things happen for you? Does Jesus get the glory when things go well? Can you see why the devil does not want you to prosper, and for life to be well with you?

## Temptations and Struggles

What about temptations and one's struggles with habitual sins, especially, those that people have seen practised by their own parents and or grandparents, and other family members?

Satan hasn't changed. He is still the father of lies and the deceiver of the brethren. His tactics haven't changed. His aim and desire is the same and he continues to operate the same way. He still tempts people. His weapons have not changed. His approach, his attacks, his tricks and lies, his ways of bringing people into bondage haven't changed. Further to this, he does not wait for you to become born again to tempt you. He starts the day you are born. Read the Gospel of John, "*They answered and said to him,*

*'You were completely born in sins, and are you teaching us?' And they cast him out."* (John 9:34)

However, the Word also says,

> *"Blessed is the man who endures temptation; for when he has been approved, he will receive the crown of life which the Lord has promised to those who love Him. Let no one say when he is tempted, 'I am tempted by God'; for God cannot be tempted by evil, nor does He Himself tempt anyone. But each one is tempted when he is drawn away by his own desires and enticed. Then, when desire has conceived, it gives birth to sin; and sin, when it is full-grown, brings forth death."* (James 1:12-15)

Temptations from the devil were always there in your life, even from when you were a toddler. If for some reason, you became entangled with a particular sin before becoming born again, you can overcome and defeat that sin. You can defeat it through Jesus Christ. You can overcome it, leave it behind, and go on to live a clean life before God and man. It is not a 'generational curse'. It is sin! Even if it seems a similar sin to that your forefathers practised.

Yes, even though, you may have been influenced by the same demons, curses of your forefathers, and may have been affected by the same environment they lived in; that does not mean that you cannot be delivered totally from sin and iniquity. It does not mean that you have to succumb to them and live with them for the rest of your life. You are an overcomer!

Anything that has become habitual and is still with you is what it is -- a habitual sin that you need to overcome and be set free of. If you are struggling with a certain habitual sin -- sin is sin – so must be overcome and conquered. Please understand that as long as you are in this flesh, as long as you are living on this earth, Satan will take advantage of any opportunity he is given, to tempt you. However, know this also, that as long as you are born again, you have power and authority to defeat Satan in your life. You have the power to overcome any sin, any habit, and to break any hold that the devil has on you. The Word says, "*Behold, I give you the authority to trample on serpents and scorpions, and over all the power of the enemy, and nothing shall by any means hurt you.*" (Luke 10:19) as well, "*For sin shall not have dominion over you, for you are not under law but under grace.*" (Romans 6:14) Hallelujah! If you want to learn more about overcoming Satan and his temptations, to develop a greater, more intimate relationship with the Lord, read my book, 'The Power is Yours'.

Let me add something right now that has to do with punishment for sin, that is very important for you to keep in mind. The pronouncement of God upon the children of Israel, who had gone after and worshipped idols, is not upon you. God is not punishing you for the sins of your forefathers. Therefore, any sin that your forefathers practised, that you may be struggling with at present, is not God's punishment upon you. You can defeat that enemy! I must reiterate -- your enemy is not, a 'generational curse'. Your only enemy is every evil spirit sent from hell against you. If you believe that you have allowed the devil to have a stronghold in your life because you accepted some wrong teachings, pray this prayer to the Lord:

> "*Father God, in the name of Jesus Christ my Lord and my Saviour, I repent for accepting any wrong teachings and beliefs, that I, as a born again child of God, am 'generationally cursed.' I renounce the thought, this wrong belief, and every word that came out of my mouth declaring that I was 'generationally cursed.' Father God, please forgive me. I ask that You remove every operation of Satan and the results of this belief from my life. I am free in Jesus' name!*

Father, from now on, I go forward in the name
that is above all names, Jesus Christ. I have power
and authority to overcome the enemy and I will
overcome to the very end. I have been redeemed by
the blood of Jesus Christ which cleanses me of all
sin and unrighteousness, and of all sicknesses and
diseases. The blood of Jesus Christ has power over
me and my life.

Father God, You are my Father, and all my
inheritance comes from you, not from anyone else. I
have inherited eternal life, abundant life, everlasting
joy and happiness, and the peace of God that passes
human understanding. Life is mine. I will serve
You with gladness and joy, peace and happiness.
You will glorify Yourself in and through me. All
praise and honour go to Your name, oh Lord, my
God. I pray all of this in the name of Jesus Christ,
my Lord. Amen."

# 8

## WHY CURSES?

*"...I shall seem to be a deceiver to him; and*
*I shall bring a curse on myself and not a*
*blessing."*
(Genesis 27:2)

What is a curse? Simply put, curses are any evil that comes upon people. What is the cause of a curse and what brings it upon people? Curses are the result of sin. If you went right back to the beginning of creation; you would see that the curse was the result of the fall of man. When man disobeyed God, curses came upon him. It is not God's desire for curses to come upon anyone. He never planned to bring evil on people. God is not the author of evil. However, He allows evil to take place. Why is that?

Have you ever heard the saying, *"What you sow, you will reap?"* (Galatians 6:7, 8) Well, that is exactly it. What you plant, you will reap. You cannot plant oranges and expect apples. It just won't happen. So why does a person expect to plant sin and receive righteousness? Why does one anticipate God's blessing when one lives like the devil? While someone practices sin and lives in the devil's domain, why do they think that God will protect them? Why does a person hope for riches when they steal from God's account? As well, why, when the offering plate comes around, do people keep back the tithe which belongs to God? (Malachi 3:8–11; Matthew 23:23; Luke 11:42) God's law says, "*What you sow, you will reap.*" Now, I am about to illuminate to you how to free yourself from a particular place that you may be in today. It is a bit lengthy and detailed, so have patience as you read. Although, I believe that you will be freed and blessed by what you are about to learn or be reminded of.

## Sowing and Reaping

Every single one of us, if we think about it, believes that this saying, "What you sow, you will reap," is true. People do not doubt it or think that it is untrue. After all, God spoke it. God also asked us to give (or sow) the tithe, didn't He? Why is it that some people do not believe that Christians should tithe today? "Oh, Pastor David, that is Old Testament! That is for the Levites. It is of the Law. It is only for Israel. It is clear in the Bible that Christians should not tithe." Well, what if God were to say to you, "If that is what you believe, then all the blessings of the Old Testament are not for you either. They all belong to Israel not to Christians…" How would you react? Think about it. If tithing is for the Old Testament people only, then the blessing from Malachi 3:10, 11 is not for you either. " '*And try Me now in this,' Says the Lord of hosts, 'If I will not open for you the windows of heaven and pour out for you such blessing…. And I will rebuke the devourer for your sakes….* "

What do you think?

That blessing is attached to the tithe! God will *open His windows of Heaven and pour out a blessing* upon you if you tithe. He will also *rebuke the thief* who is robbing you of your wealth, health and wholeness, if you tithe. You cannot rob God of the tithe and then expect Him to give the blessing that is connected to it. Can you? Should you? If so why?

Those who tithe have the legal and God given right to expect to receive the blessing of Malachi 3:10, and 11. It is theirs! When I myself consider this commandment in Malachi, I think to myself, "I would be foolish not to tithe. If God is going to pour out a blessing upon me and rebuke Satan on my behalf when I tithe; why would I act foolishly by not giving the tithe?" Follow me in this. Think about it. This blessing legally belongs to you because you have given the tithe. You have the God-given legal right to ask the Lord to pour out blessings upon you, and to stop Satan in his tracks when he comes to trouble your life!

## He Was Made a Curse

"But, Pastor Ramiah, Jesus Christ was made a curse for me so that Abraham's blessing would be mine. Look at it."

> *"Christ has redeemed us from the curse of the law, having become a curse for us (for it is written, 'Cursed is everyone who hangs on a tree', that the blessing of Abraham might come upon the Gentiles in Christ Jesus, that we might receive the promise of the Spirit through faith."* (Galatians 3:13, 14)

"You see that Pastor David? Jesus Christ was made a curse for me when He was crucified, and Abraham's blessing then came onto us Christians so we receive that promise through faith." It is true. Abraham's blessing did come onto Christians, is for Christians, and is received by faith. You do not see Abraham's blessing with your naked eye, do you? No, you see it with the eyes of faith. You receive it through your faith.

Let's look at something. When Abraham came back from the battle and brought back his nephew Lot and all the other people, who was it that met him on the way? If you said Melchizedek, you are correct.

*"For this Melchizedek, king of Salem, priest of the Most High God, who met Abraham returning from the slaughter of the kings and blessed him, to whom also Abraham gave a tenth part of all, first being translated 'king of righteousness,' and then also king of Salem, meaning 'king of peace,' without father, without mother, without genealogy, having neither beginning of days nor end of life, but made like the Son of God, remains a priest continually."*
(Hebrews 7:1–3)

This man, Melchizedek, was a full representation of Jesus Christ our Lord. Look at his titles, "King of Righteousness, and King of Salem, meaning King of Peace." This same man met Abraham after he had won a great battle, and was returning home. When Abraham saw him, without question Abraham gave him a tithe - 10 % of all the material goods that he had taken from the Kings whom he had defeated. Whether it was gold, silver, clothing, sheep, goats, and donkeys, Abraham gave 10 % of it all to Melchizedek who represented Jesus Christ. *"The Lord has sworn and will not relent, 'You are a priest forever according to the order of Melchizedek.'"* (Psalm 110:4)

Jesus Christ is of the priesthood of Melchizedek. Notice that this is not the Levitical or Aaronic priesthood under which Moses gave the Law. It is the order of Melchizedek, or the priesthood of Melchizedek, who remains a priest *continually.*

*"As He also says in another place: 'You are a priest forever according to the order of Melchizedek' who, in the days of His flesh, when He had offered up prayers and supplications, with vehement cries and tears to Him who was able to save Him from death, and was heard because of His godly fear, though He was a Son, yet He learned obedience by the things which He suffered. And having been perfected, He became the author of eternal salvation to all who*

*obey Him, called by God as High Priest 'according
to the order of Melchizedek,' of whom we have much
to say, and hard to explain, since you have become
dull of hearing."* (Hebrews 5:6–11)

'*In the order of*', or '*according to the priesthood of Melchizedek*',
tithing began. It is the very first place that tithing is mentioned
in the Bible. It is important that we realize tithing started under
the Melchizedek priesthood. It did not start under the Levitical
or Aaronic priesthood. It was later added to the Law to supply
the needs of the Priests and Levites and their families. This is very
important to remember.

Since Jesus is of the priesthood of Melchizedek which is
perpetual, why would we assume that tithing ceased? Is it because
we are under a New Covenant, which was made in and through
Jesus Christ -- the author and finisher of our faith? Abraham was
the first person recorded in the Bible to give the tithe freely. He
was not asked for it. Neither was it demanded of him. *He gave it to
the man who was the full representation of Jesus Christ*. Melchizedek,
the full representation of Jesus Christ our Lord, blessed Abraham.
*The representative blessed the one who gave the tithe.*

*"Then Melchizedek king of Salem brought out bread
and wine; he was the priest of God Most High.
And he blessed him and said: 'Blessed be Abram of
God Most High, Possessor of heaven and earth; and
blessed be God Most High, Who has delivered your
enemies into your hand.' And he gave him a tithe
of all."* (Genesis 14:18–20)

Abraham was still called Abram at this time.

Melchizedek pulled out bread and wine. What did he do with
it? He gave it to Abraham, of course. How did he give it to him,
I wonder? Do you think that perhaps he broke bread with him?
From the Scripture verse, we are told that he gave the tithe after
breaking bread. The Bible specifically stressed, *"He was the priest of*

*God Most High.*" I do not think that Abraham was hungry. Before Abraham went to war, he would have prepared and planned to feed himself and his army. He would have brought enough food for everybody. Furthermore, he had all the food he took from the armies he had destroyed. He didn't need food!

I do not believe this bread and wine was for an entire army. This was for '*the chosen of God' Abram*. It was for Melchizedek and Abram to break bread together. What form that took I do not know, but the next time we hear of another priest breaking bread with His own, was when the High Priest, Jesus Christ, broke bread with His disciples. Do you see the connection?

> "*When the hour had come, He sat down, and the twelve apostles with Him. Then He said to them, 'With fervent desire I have desired to eat this Passover with you before I suffer; for I say to you, I will no longer eat of it until it is fulfilled in the kingdom of God.' Then He took the cup, and gave thanks, and said, 'Take this and divide it among yourselves; for I say to you, I will not drink of the fruit of the vine until the kingdom of God comes.' And He took bread, gave thanks and broke it, and gave it to them, saying, 'This is My body which is given for you; do this in remembrance of Me.' Likewise He also took the cup after supper, saying, 'This cup is the new covenant in My blood, which is shed for you.'*"
> (Luke 22:14-19)

Now that we have made the connection between Melchizedek and Jesus, and since we see that Melchizedek, as the full representative of Jesus Christ, received the tithe from Abram on behalf of Jesus, shouldn't the disciples of the High Priest give Him the tithe? Should not Jesus Christ receive tithes from us His followers?

Abram received bread and wine from Melchizedek in a form of celebration after his victory. The disciples received bread and wine (fruit of the vine) from the Lord in celebrating and instituting the New Covenant. Abram gave a tithe, 10% of all the material goods he won in battle; of all by which he was increased, to Melchizedek, the priest of God, after they broke bread together. Shouldn't the followers of Jesus Christ give Him the Tithe? Our present time for tithing is after the first Communion that Jesus had with His disciples.

"But Pastor Ramiah, Jesus did not ask His disciples for the tithe! He could have taken a tithe from them that night." You are absolutely correct! He could have, but was that night about tithing or was it about instituting the New Covenant? Wasn't that night about what Jesus was going to do for you and me on a cross? **Tithing had already been instituted between Jesus' representative Melchizedek, and Abram, your representative and mine**. Jesus didn't need to do it again. The disciples under the Mosaic Law were already giving their tithes at the temple. He didn't need to teach them about it all over again. So there was no reason for Jesus to tell them about it, or remind them to give it. He did not have to collect a tithe and record it for our benefit either. It was already there; instituted and practised.

Were the disciples there when Jesus spoke these words? "*Woe to you, scribes and Pharisees, hypocrites! For you pay tithe of mint and anise and cummin, and have neglected the weightier matters of the law: justice and mercy and faith. These you ought to have done, without leaving the others undone.*" (Matthew 23:23) Did the Pharisees hear Him say, "*These you ought to have done, without leaving the others undone.*"? Furthermore, was this teaching of Jesus for the scribes and Pharisees, as well as the disciples? Since the answer is, "Yes" each time. If Jesus did not want His disciples to tithe; He would have told them so. Don't you agree? Well, you might say, "That is the only place that it is mentioned in the Gospels about tithing. So I am not sure that is enough to say that Christians should tithe."

Let us see then. Paul mentioned something about tithing. Could this be another place that we can look at and say we have more proof in the New Testament? Let's take a look. I have chosen the Amplified Bible, so that we may be able to have a clearer understanding of what Paul is saying.

> "For this Melchizedek, king of Salem [and] priest of the Most High God, met Abraham as he returned from the slaughter of the kings and blessed him, and Abraham gave to him a tenth portion of all [the spoil]. He is primarily, as his name when translated indicates, king of righteousness, and then he is also king of Salem, which means king of peace."
> (Hebrews 7:1, 2 Amplified)

First, Paul establishes in verses one and two that Melchizedek was a priest of God, who met Abram, blessed him, and received a tithe from him. "*Without [record of] father or mother or ancestral line, neither with beginning of days nor ending of life, but, resembling the Son of God, he continues to be a priest without interruption and without successor.*" (Hebrews 7:3 Amplified) Second, he tells us in verse three that Melchizedek was like Jesus Christ our Lord, and that he remains a priest continually.

> "Now observe and consider how great [a personage] this was to whom even Abraham the patriarch gave a tenth [the topmost or the pick of the heap] of the spoils. And it is true that those descendants of Levi who are charged with the priestly office are commanded in the Law to take tithes from the people — which means, from their brethren—though these have descended from Abraham." (Hebrews 7:4, 5 Amplified)

Third, he shows us that the Levites received tithes from their brothers -- children of Abraham to whom the promises were made. He tries very hard to show that those who were to receive the promises — blessings, gave the tithe and were supposed to give it. We are also beneficiaries of the promises and blessings of God. So again, should we not give the tithe?

> *"But this person who has not their Levitical ancestry received tithes from Abraham [himself] and blessed him who possessed the promises [of God]. Yet it is beyond all contradiction that it is the lesser person who is blessed by the greater one."* (Hebrews 7:6, 7 Amplified)

Fourth, Paul specifies in verses six and seven that Melchizedek, who *was not a Levite,* received a tithe from Abraham. Thus, we know that this was when tithing was instituted. He makes a clear distinction between tithing in the Mosaic Law, and tithing according to this relationship between Melchizedek and Abraham. Remember, as *the full representation of Jesus Christ,* he received this tithe from Abraham and blessed him on behalf of the Lord. Paul made the effort for a reason, which was to demonstrate that Melchizedek who blessed Abraham was greater than he was.

> *"Furthermore, here [in the Levitical priesthood] tithes are received by men who are subject to death; while there [in the case of Melchizedek], they are received by one of whom it is testified that he lives [perpetually]."* (Hebrews 7:8 Amplified)

Fifth, in verse eight, Paul stressed the point of how both tithes were received. This is a remarkable verse of Scripture regarding the tithe. Paul wrote that the Levites who received the tithes according to the Law, die. Other Levites soon take their place and continue to receive the tithe according to the Law. However, in Melchizedek's case, he doesn't die! Therefore, he is never replaced. The representative of Jesus Christ never dies. Neither does Jesus Christ our Lord die. They live on forever! Thus, the custom, the practice; the unwritten law of giving the tithe according to Melchizedek's priesthood of which Jesus Christ our Lord is the

High Priest, does not die either. Neither do the blessings that come with the practice of giving the tithe, die.

Paul shows us that the Levites received tithes — plural. He also says that in the case of Melchizedek, '*they are received*'. What does he mean they are received? In grammatical terms, the present tense is used for things that never change and go on forever. The Bible tells us that Abraham gave '*a*' tithe to Melchizedek. So, when Paul says, '*they*' are received, what does he mean? He is obviously speaking of tithes, not a single tithe. Therefore, he is not speaking *only* of the tithe that Melchizedek received from Abraham when Abraham returned from the Battle. He is talking about Melchizedek's Priestly Order of which Jesus Christ is, which is a Priesthood that has no end. *"For it is evident that our Lord arose from Judah of which tribe Moses spoke nothing concerning priesthood."* (Hebrews 7:14-16) Paul was clarifying the ongoing Priesthood of our Lord Jesus Christ so that the tithe is continuously received.

*"It is yet far more evident if, in the likeness of Melchizedek, there arises another priest who has come, not according to the law of a fleshly commandment, but according to the power of an endless life. For He testifies: 'You are a priest forever according to the order of Melchizedek.'"* (Hebrews 7:14–16 Amplified) Jesus Christ is not only a priest *according to the Order of Melchizedek*, but He is **the High Priest** according to the Order of Melchizedek so that according to the Order of Melchizedek, our Lord and Saviour receives the tithes, '*them*' from Christians to whom promises were made according to the New Covenant. As Abraham received the promises and gave the tithe; as well, his children who received the promises through Abraham gave the tithe, so too, you and I must do likewise. Christians are asked to give the tithe to our High Priest, Jesus Christ. Not according to the Law, but according to the Order or in the fashion of which Melchizedek received it -- freely from the heart. Yes, it is still a tithe and yes, it is freely given.

Why did Paul preach so much about tithing, about Melchizedek being like Jesus, Abraham giving the tithe, and his children continuing to give the tithe according to the Law? Why did he place so much stress on it?

> *"Now this is the main point of the things we are saying: We have such a High Priest, who is seated at the right hand of the throne of the Majesty in the heavens, a Minister of the sanctuary and of the true tabernacle which the Lord erected, and not man. For every high priest is appointed to offer both gifts and sacrifices. Therefore it is necessary that this One also have something to offer."* (Hebrews 8:1-3)

Do you agree with Paul that Jesus Christ our Lord and High Priest should have something to offer to God our Father on our behalf? He paid a debt He did not owe, for us to have abundant life. This was the biggest gift of all time.... For us, He gave His life — His all. He laid down His Godhead when He came to earth as a baby to take on human form. Then, He even gave that life back to the Father on our behalf. The ultimate sacrifice; the very thing that He came on earth to do and to fulfill, the full price -- 100% paid for you and for me -- He gave His life. Why is it so difficult for some Christians to give 10% of their increase; their wages, of their wealth to God?

Why do Christians today complain about giving a tithe? Of only 10 % of what we earn? Why do most of the people who do not give tithes, fight the concept of tithing so much? Is it perhaps because they love their money more than their God? Is it that their money is closer to their hearts than God is? Isn't it also because their security is in their money and not in God? On the other hand, there are Christians who love God so much, but they have never been taught the truth about tithing. So as soon as they get the truth, they cannot wait to take their tithe to church.

What can we conclude? Tithing is still to be practised in our day. In the teachings of both Paul and our Lord Jesus, we have seen that if a person is keeping back the tithe or 10% of their wages, they 'are robbing' God. Does this bring a curse upon them? You be the judge. *"Will a man rob God? Yet you have robbed Me! But you say, 'In what way have we robbed You?' In tithes and offerings. You are cursed with a curse, for you have robbed Me, even this whole nation."* (Malachi 3:8, 9) Wow! If you happen to be someone who does not tithe because you did not understand that you had to give it, acknowledge this to the Lord. Repent of robbing God of His money and ask Him for forgiveness. Take the Lord's money to your church where it belongs. You will be freed from any curse related to robbing God of His tithe.

Keep this in mind. Meditate on it in your heart.

> " *'Bring all the tithes into the storehouse, That there may be food in My house, And try Me now in this,' Says the Lord of hosts, 'If I will not open for you the windows of heaven and pour out for you such blessing that there will not be room enough to receive it. 'And I will rebuke the devourer for your sakes, So that he will not destroy the fruit of your ground, nor shall the vine fail to bear fruit for you in the field,... 'And all nations will call you blessed, for you will be a delightful land,' Says the Lord of hosts.* "
> (Malachi 3:10-12)

Don't you want this kind of great blessing that God is talking about here in Malachi? Dear child of God, this blessing is specifically related to the tithe. Give to God His tithe, and this blessing related to tithing will be yours.

Furthermore, when He says that He will *'rebuke the devourer',* who is the devourer? It is Satan! The devil is the one who steals, kills and destroys. When you give to the Lord His tithe, He will stop the devil from stealing from you. God will deliver you from Satan's hands. If there is such a curse as in Malachi 3:9 upon your life, God will remove it.

Father God, I dedicate my life to live in obedience to every word of Yours. I will give You what belongs to You and I will not rob You of your tithe. I will honour time that is set apart for You like days of worship, for prayer and study of Your word, and I will use my gifts and talents to glorify Your name and to be a blessing to people. I commit myself now to be a doer of Your word and not just a hearer of it. I will walk in all Your ways as You guide me by Your Holy Spirit and give me the strength and power to do so. Dear God my Father, I ask You to rebuke Satan for stealing my wealth, my health and my happiness from me. Cause Your blessing that is in and upon my life to manifest in my life in abundance. I will give You the praise and the glory for it. I ask all this in Jesus' name. Amen.

# 9

## TRUE CONFESSION

*"Have faith in God. For assuredly, I say to*
*you, whoever… does not doubt in his heart,*
*but believes that those things he says will be*
*done, he will have whatever he says.'"*
(Mark 11:22-23)

I had a discussion with a friend of mine not too long ago. Our discussion demonstrated to me once again, how prevalent this teaching is in the Body of Christ, and that generational curses have passed on from ungodly forefathers to Christians. My friend wanted me to understand that a 'generational curse' that passed on to a Christian, is not the one spoken of in Exodus 20:5. He explained, "This is the curse of the fathers which they suffered such as drunkenness. It passed on into the flesh of a Christian because a person still carries the sin nature in their flesh. That is where the curse passes into and that is why people are tempted and struggle with sins of their fathers." We didn't have enough time for much discussion as we were in his office and he had to leave for an appointment. I too had to be on my way. So we didn't discuss it any further. It was left for another time. This friend of mine and I have often discussed many subjects of the Bible. Thus, many times we have had so much revealed to us by the Holy Spirit.

Well, in light of the previous discussion what do you think? Do you believe that this is true? Do you believe that the generational curse -- evil practices, habits and bondages of your forefathers have managed to be passed on to you in your flesh? We have discussed this in past chapters so I believe that by this time, you have a better understanding of the subject. You know that this didn't happen and couldn't. For the sake of giving more clarity to our discussion and to remove any further doubt, I have chosen to elaborate more on this. In order to do so, we once again need to look at Exodus. What really is the truth behind it all? How can we further prove that generational curses have not passed on to Christians from their forefathers? We need to know the truth because *"And you shall know the truth, and the truth shall make you free."*(John 8:32)

*Let us, therefore, look first at Exodus.*

*"You shall not make for yourself a carved image— any likeness of anything that is in heaven above, or that is in the earth beneath, or that is in the water under the earth; you shall not bow down to them nor serve them. For I, the Lord your God, am a jealous God, visiting the iniquity of the fathers upon the children to the third and fourth generations of those who hate Me, but showing mercy to thousands, to those who love Me and keep My commandments. "*(Exodus 20:4-6)

Why scholars have used this portion of Scripture to teach Christians that curses -- sins, iniquities and transgressions and whatever else have passed on to them is unbelievable. The truth is that generational curses have not passed on to Christians! It just cannot happen. At the end of it all, we have to seek the truth. Only the truth matters, not logic -- not 2 + 2 = 4.... God's ways are higher than ours. "*His thoughts are higher than our thoughts.*" (Isaiah 55:9) We must not take the things of God and 'add them up' using man's addition system. It will not work.

Here is something that many Christians have failed to understand: "*For as by one man's disobedience many were made sinners, so by the obedience of one shall many be made righteous.*" (Romans 5:19) By Adam's sin, we were all made sinners. By the obedience of Christ, though, when we were saved, we were made righteous. That tells me that the sin of Adam, the curse of Adam, -- sin, transgressions, iniquities, evil practices – whatever you desire to call them were all removed in the death and resurrection of Jesus Christ. That includes any generational curse -- any transgression and iniquity of our forefathers. **Gone!** These are done away with, in Jesus Christ. Look closely at what Paul says here in Romans. "*For if by one man's offence death reigned by one; much more they which receive abundance of grace and of the gift of righteousness shall reign in life by one, Jesus Christ.*" (Romans 5:17) Through the sins of Adam, we were all bound to sin, iniquity and transgression. Similarly, *before* you became born again, every kind of curse, which was passed on to you had you in its grips. There was no way out for you. You were bound, controlled, defeated, lost, dying, and on your way to hell.

However, let us give thanks to God Almighty. The moment you were born again, every sin and every curse ended with Jesus Christ! They were removed and buried with Him. You were set free! Go ahead and shout, "Hallelujah!" Then we must go back again to this Scripture, "*Or do you not know that as many of us as were baptized into Christ Jesus were baptized into His death? Therefore we were buried with Him through baptism into death, that just as Christ was raised from the dead by the glory of the Father, even so we also should walk in newness of life.*" (Romans 6:3, 4) If you were buried with Jesus Christ then you had to have died with Him. If you died with Jesus, then your sins and transgressions were nailed to the cross with Him. When you were buried with Him in water baptism, all those transgressions and all curses were buried with you, in Christ Jesus. While you were buried with Him, it also means that you were raised with Him. **Since He lives, you live!**

## The Dead Have No Inheritance

We have already seen that if you, as a person died, you would be buried. You would have lost all your inheritance that was coming to you from your parents. There would no longer be any expectation of receiving anything from them ever again. There is nothing that they could ever do for you anymore. That would be it — the end. In Jesus Christ, spiritually speaking, you died to your parents. You were then born again. You have a new life. You moved out of their lives. You were changed. You moved from your previous home to a new one. You live in God's house. You received a new Father -- God! You also received a new family – the Body of Christ. Additionally, you have a new inheritance through the New Covenant that Christ Jesus gave to you. Your strength, your overcoming power and your deliverance are now in Christ Jesus. You reign, live, move and have your being in Jesus Christ.

You know, all of God's people should be smart enough to give God credit for what He has done for them, and for what He is doing for them now. They should not give any credit to the devil for what he cannot do. Philippians 4:13 says, "*I can do all things through Christ who strengthens me.*" You can totally trust God that when He washed you in His own blood and made you clean from all your sins, that indeed He made you clean of *all* your sins! Psalm 51:7 states, "*wash me and I shall be whiter than snow.*" This is how much God purifies us.

Let's look at Isaiah "*Surely He has borne our griefs and carried our sorrows; yet we esteemed Him stricken, smitten by God, and afflicted. But He was wounded for our transgressions, He was bruised for our iniquities; the chastisement for our peace was upon Him, and by His stripes we are healed.*" (Isaiah 53:4, 5) This was prophesied even before the New Testament times opened at Jesus' birth. If

Jesus was wounded, beaten and ill-treated for your transgressions; if He suffered for your iniquities; then He paid for all our sins already, didn't He? Moreover, since **He was punished for your transgressions**, your sins and iniquities, is God going to punish you all over again for them? Would God be right to do that? If Jesus took all your iniquities to the cross, how could you still have them? How could you have inherited curses of any kind in you; in your flesh or anywhere else in your life? Jesus bore them. He carried them away with Him. He suffered, and He died. He was punished for all your sins, transgressions, iniquities and curses. That is why it says: "*Christ has redeemed us from the curse of the law, having become a curse for us (for it is written, 'Cursed is everyone who hangs on a tree'*"). (Galatians 3:13)

**To redeem** means to pay in full for something that is being redeemed. You cannot redeem your diamond ring from the pawn shop without paying the full amount that you owed. You have to pay the shop owner the full amount of money that you received, and agreed to pay back. When you redeem your jewelry, you do not expect it to be damaged. You do not anticipate that the shop owner would take away from it or add to it, do you? Well then, why is it that God's people would believe that God, who paid the full redemption price for us, would not take us back in full in His perfection? Why would He give us back our old selves with all the sins, transgressions, iniquities and curses of our forefathers? That wouldn't make sense at all would it?

Yes, God accepted you just the way you were with all your sins, iniquities, curses and everything that you *had*. Then, He washed you thoroughly with the blood of His Son, Jesus Christ. You were thus made totally clean, at that very moment when you accepted Jesus Christ as your Lord and Saviour! The blood of Jesus Christ never loses its power. It is also impossible for you to enter heaven with any sin on you. It does not make sense that if you paid the full price for something, you would take along with it something extra that you didn't want, need, or pay for. Worse yet, if you took anything that you didn't pay for, you are a thief! Allow me to let you in on something that is not such a big secret. My God is not a thief. He does not take what does not belong to Him. Therefore, if He paid for you, which He did; He will not take you and all your forefather's sins, transgressions, or curses with you. The Bible says that He nailed them together with Jesus on to the Cross. Praise the Lord!

God not only brought you back, but also *"made you a new creature in Christ Jesus"* (II Corinthians 5:17) with the death and resurrection of His only begotten Son, Jesus Christ. This meant, He exchanged His life, for your old, sinful, dead, and condemned to hell life. He took that old life of yours and everything with it and nailed it to the cross. Furthermore, when they placed Him in the tomb, your old life was placed there too! Jesus left it there. Why should He bring anything of the old back? Then, He gave you His life -- Jesus' Life. **There is no curse in the Life of Christ!** Do you know why some Christians do not understand this truth? And why they do not understand that generational curses could not have passed on to your new Life? **They took faith out of their reasoning.** Faith was put aside in their assumptions and opinions.

However, it is only by faith that *"we live, move and have our being"* (Acts 17:28) in Christ Jesus. It is only our faith in Him that tells us that we have new life. Faith in the Lord demonstrates to us that we do not have to believe a lie. Faith is what causes us to believe the truth of the Gospel -- the good news. Faith causes me to believe that God saved me and cleansed me of all my sins, and that He made me a *new creation*. Why do I have to add to or take away from the Word of God when what it says is true? If I go by the philosophies and doctrines of man, that is exactly what I will do. I will add to or take away from the Word of God. If I go by what doctors and scientists say, and I try to justify it with Scripture, I have added to the Word of God. God's Word does not need confirmation or agreement from doctors or scientists to be true. His word is always true. What God says is how and what it is.

When God said that you were made a new creation, then that is what you have been made. He said that the old person that you were, passed away. Since God said so, it is so. He said that *all things* about you, concerning you, and of you, have been made new. *"Therefore, from now on, we regard no one according to the flesh. Even though we have known Christ according to the flesh, yet now we know Him thus no longer. Therefore, if anyone is in Christ, he is a new creation; old things have passed away; behold, all things have become new."* (II Corinthians 5:16, 17) With the wisdom that only comes from God, the Apostle Paul made the decision not to look at any Christian according to the flesh. He looked at them according to the Spirit. Why? Because they had become a new creation! Above all, as Paul had been a great persecutor of Christians and was knocked down and blinded on the road to Damascus to meet up with Jesus; he understood what it meant to be a new creation much more than most people do. Listen, if God, through the Apostle Paul, says that you are a new creation, then that is what you are! He is talking about you. He tells us that everything about you has passed away, and has been done away with. It is gone. Everything about you and concerning you from the moment of your new birth is new.

Furthermore, God says that you are righteous. *"For He made Him who knew no sin to be sin for us, that we might become the righteousness of God in Him."* (II Corinthians 5:21) You became 'the righteousness of God' the very moment that you became His child, at your new birth. You can read more about this in my book, 'What You Weren't Told about Righteousness'.

## Curse versus Temptation

The argument that I have heard and may hear again, is that the curse of your forefathers passed into your flesh. Therefore, to rid yourself of it, you may have been told to cut it off you through special prayers and that you need to literally remove it by cutting off each curse by speaking to each one. I have nothing against anyone praying such a prayer. However, the way people talk is as if God was not able to do this when He redeemed you.

This is a walk of faith not of your works! It is not by your works that you are saved. It is not by an act of some preacher, pastor, evangelist or other minister praying for you. It is by one act! It was the death and the resurrection of Jesus Christ that did it. "But Pastor David, you have to apply that to your life!" I agree. Only receive Christ Jesus as your Lord and Saviour. Change your thinking, your desire and emotions by the renewing of your mind. Fill your heart and mind with the Word of God every day. Worship and praise Him every day. Pray always, fast from time to time, and fellowship with other believers in a church that preaches the Bible. If you do, you will not satisfy the desires of your flesh, and you will not obey its cravings.

People wrongly associate temptation with curses. When you are tempted by the devil, it is not because you are under a curse or that you are cursed. Was Jesus tempted? Was He tempted because He was cursed? It is not a curse, which came from your forefathers that causes you to be tempted. Neither is it the curses of your forefathers that you struggle with in your Christian life. No, *"For we wrestle... against principalities, against powers, against the rulers of the darkness of this world, against spiritual wickedness in high places."* (Ephesians 6:12) Then again, *"For the weapons of our warfare are not carnal but mighty in God for pulling down strongholds, casting down arguments and every high thing that exalts itself against the knowledge of God, bringing every thought into captivity to the obedience of Christ, and being ready to punish all disobedience when your obedience is fulfilled."* (2 Corinthians 10:4–6)

Your battle is against Satan and his host of evil spirits. This is what you are fighting against. They are the ones who have come against you and provoked you to sin -- not your forefathers' curses. Those spirits are the ones that are doing everything possible to bring you into captivity and to keep you there. Furthermore, these evil spirits are also using the lie that was told to you, "Generational curses have passed on to you…" If you believe that lie, then Satan already has a foothold in your life. Repent for receiving that lie and rebuke it, and you will be freed immediately in the name of Jesus Christ.

If you believe the lie that you have a curse of your forefathers upon your life, Satan will make sure that you continue to believe that. He is going to try you even more in that area. He is going to tempt you, trip you up, push your buttons, and do everything possible to make you fall and stay fallen, and to make you believe that you have a 'generational curse'. If you can understand in your heart that you have overcome Satan by the blood of Jesus Christ, and by your testimony, you will win every time. You are not fighting a generational curse. You are fighting the devil. It is a lie that you have to live with whatever you are struggling with. You can overcome it! Jesus is able to give you the victory and to lead you to triumph. *"And they overcame him by the blood of the Lamb, and by the word of their testimony; and they loved not their lives unto the death."* (Revelation 12:11)

What is causing people to have problems? It is not, 'generational curses'. It is not some sin of their forefathers. It is possible that something which your father did in his life time, may affect you negatively. For example, if he wasted all his earnings on drugs or alcohol, you have no money or inheritance to look forward to. If your parents died and left you with a house, which was not paid off, you have to live with that debt. However, it is not true that because your parents or their parents have committed atrocious sins, you have to pay for them.

What is your testimony going to be? Are you going to testify that you have a curse? Will you confess that the curse of your grandfather's drunkenness is in your flesh? Or will you confess, "I have overcome the curse of drunkenness by the blood of Jesus Christ"? Will you testify that the curse of your great grandfather's adultery is in your flesh? Or will you confess that you are more than a conqueror in Christ Jesus? Or that the curse of lust that was in your grandmother is in your flesh, or was passed on to you? Or do you testify **"Jesus Christ has washed me of all sins. I am free from every sin including the evil practices of my forefathers."** When you are tempted, will you testify, "This is the curse of the womanizing, lusting and whore mongering of my father, my grandfather, my great-grandfather, and my great-great grandfather, so I am defeated."? Or will you testify, "I will submit to God, resist the devil and he will flee from me. I will not obey the lusts of the flesh. I will not succumb to its cravings. I will walk in the Spirit and I will not satisfy the flesh. Jesus Christ is my strength. I am an Overcomer!" *"What you believe in your heart will dictate your confession. What you confess, you will have."* (See Romans10:9-10)

## You are a Winner

You are not a loser. You are a winner. God did not save you so that you should continue to sin. As a matter of fact, God forbids it. You were saved to live holy and righteously. Moreover, God has given you everything to not only defeat the enemy's attacks and lies, but also to live a Godly life. First of all, He gave you His life. He has given you His Word. He gave you His name. He gave you His Holy Spirit, His power, His strength, and His authority.

> *"Now this I say lest anyone should deceive you with persuasive words. For though I am absent in the flesh, yet I am with you in spirit, rejoicing to see your good order and the steadfastness of your faith in Christ. As you **therefore have received Christ Jesus the Lord, so walk in Him, rooted and built up in Him and established in the faith,** as you have been taught, abounding in it with thanksgiving. Beware lest anyone cheat you through philosophy and empty deceit, according to the tradition of men, according to the basic principles of the world, and not according to Christ. **For in Him dwells all the fullness of the Godhead bodily; and you are complete in Him,** who is*

*the head of all principality and power. In Him you were also circumcised with the circumcision made without hands, by putting off the body of the sins of the flesh, by the circumcision of Christ, buried with Him in baptism, in which you also were raised with Him through faith in the working of God, who raised Him from the dead. And you, being dead in your trespasses and the uncircumcision of your flesh,* **He has made alive together with Him, having forgiven you all trespasses, having wiped out the handwriting of requirements that was against us, which was contrary to us.** *And He has taken it out of the way, having nailed it to the cross."* (Colossians 2:4-14)

Notice that you are complete in Jesus. If you live unto Christ, you will not fulfill the desires of the flesh. This is the secret to overcoming the enemy. The key to defeating Satan in your life is obedience to Christ Jesus. It is living to please Him and not living to please the self. The secret to overcoming and defeating the devil is to allow Christ to live in and through you on a daily basis. *"For if, when we were enemies, we were reconciled to God by the death of his Son, much more, being reconciled, we shall be saved by his life."* (Romans 5:10) As well, *"No weapon formed against you shall prosper, and every tongue which rises against you in judgment You shall condemn. This is the heritage of the servants of the Lord, and their righteousness is from Me," Says the Lord."* (Isaiah 54:17) That's right my friend! This is your **inheritance in Isaiah 54:17, not curses**. Your inheritance comes from God.

What is in your heart? In Proverbs 23:7 we read, *"For as he thinks in his heart, so is he…"* Jesus also said, *"A good man out of the good treasure of his heart brings forth good; and an evil man out of the evil treasure of his heart brings forth evil. For out of the abundance of the heart his mouth speaks."* (Luke 6:45) And here also: *"So Jesus answered and said to them, 'Have faith in God. For assuredly, I say to you, whoever says to this mountain, 'Be removed and be cast into the sea,' and does not doubt in his heart, but believes that those things he says will be done, he will have whatever he says."* (Mark 11:22-23)

Have you been thinking and believing that you have, 'generational curses' operating in your life? Have you said, or are you proclaiming that you have, 'generational curses'? If you have done so, you need to repent of this before the Lord right away. Ask God for forgiveness for these thoughts which you most likely declared out of your mouth. Renounce every thought, especially the words you have said about being 'generationally cursed', and you will immediately be set free. Let your confession be one that glorifies Jesus, that declares the goodness and righteousness of God working in you to bring glory to His name. Let it be a testimony that God is greater than your enemies, that God causes you to overcome evil and gives you the victory, and that you reign and move and have your being in Him and that you win every time.

> *My Father and my God, You have made me to become the righteousness of God in Christ Jesus according to 2 Corinthians 5:21, a new creation. I am not the same person that I used to be. I am brand new. I am seated at Your right hand in Jesus Christ and You have made me to be complete in Him according to Colossians 2:10. As a matter of fact, I am hidden with Christ in God according to Colossians 3:3. By your Holy Spirit, You will cause me to overcome sin and temptation. Lead me not into temptation oh dear Father, but lead me in the path of righteousness for Your name sake, in Jesus' name. Amen.*

# 10

## HE WHO SINS

*"But if a wicked man turns from all his*
*sin...,and does what is lawful and right...*
*None of the transgressions which he has*
*committed shall be remembered against*
*him..."*
(Ezekiel 18:21-22)

It is important for us to understand that sin is something we have to deal with as long as we live on this earth. Committing sin has ramifications. It therefore demands close attention. We must make every effort to deal with it. "...'*The fathers have eaten sour grapes, and the children's teeth are set on edge*?" (Ezekiel 18:2) In Exodus, God pronounced a curse upon Israel. If a father sinned, (worshipping idols,) the children would pay for it. Payment for that particular sin would go on to the fourth generation. So, down through the line of sons; from the father to his son, to that son's son, and then to this son's son, and lastly to the last son's son. It's a tongue twister isn't it? Simply stated, a man's son down to the third

grandson would pay for his particular sin. This is what is meant
by; "*The children's teeth are set on edge.*" The fathers committed
the crime, and the children did the time, or in other words, they
paid for it.

However, God changed this specific law or command, or the
foretold curse, whatever you desire to call it. He ended it when
the Lord said to Ezekiel, "*You will never use this saying ever again!*"
as well, "As I live," says the Lord God, "*you shall no longer use this
proverb in Israel.*" (Ezekiel 18:3) No longer means, "No more."
When God says no more, that is exactly what He means. If God
were to say something like this to you, what would you make of
it? Would you think, "Well, it must have been just for Ezekiel and
just for that period of time. Perhaps, God changed His mind and
this continued later."

I know, though, that you are more intelligent than that. God
is the same yesterday, today and forever. If He says that He has
changed the law, then He **has changed** it. I do not believe that if
God spoke directly to you as He spoke to Ezekiel, that you would
have believed anything else. Look at this --"*Behold, all souls are
Mine; the soul of the father as well as the soul of the son is Mine; the
soul who sins shall die.*" (Ezekiel 18:4) What is God telling us? He is
stipulating that every soul is accountable directly to God for his or
her own wrong. Every person has to have his or her own personal
relationship with the Lord.

## The Just Man

Furthermore, in Ezekiel we can read and understand a great
deal. God said:

> "*But if a man is just and does what is lawful and
> right; If he has not eaten on the mountains, nor
> lifted up his eyes to the idols of the house of Israel,
> nor defiled his neighbor's wife, nor approached a
> woman during her impurity; if he has not oppressed*

*anyone, but has restored to the debtor his pledge; has
robbed no one by violence, but has given his bread
to the hungry and covered the naked with clothing;
if he has not exacted usury nor taken any increase,
but has withdrawn his hand from iniquity and
executed true judgment between man and man; if
he has walked in My statutes and kept My judgments
faithfully— he is just; he shall surely live!' says the
Lord God."* (Ezekiel 18:5-9)

If a man practised righteousness and did good, he would be
rewarded for the good. He would live and not die. He has done
righteously. What is God showing us? The righteous man will be
rewarded for his own good. Good is not taken away from him
because of his father's past sins. This good man is rewarded because
he practises righteousness and he does the right things. God is a
rewarder of those who diligently seek Him and obey Him.

What if this righteous man, though, has a bad, sinful son?

*"If he begets a son who is a robber Or a shedder of
blood, Who does any of these things and does none
of those duties, but has eaten on the mountains or
defiled his neighbor's wife; if he has oppressed the
poor and needy, robbed by violence, not restored
the pledge, lifted his eyes to the idols, or committed
abomination; if he has exacted usury or taken
increase—shall he then live? He shall not live! If
he has done any of these abominations, he shall
surely die; his blood shall be upon him."* (Ezekiel
18:10–13)

The evil son cannot inherit a good reward from God just
because his father was a righteous man. This evil son must pay for
his own sins. This wicked son cannot be blessed just because his
father was blessed. He does not inherit blessings, but is punished
for his own sins. What if another wicked man in turn, has a son

who practises righteousness? Does his righteous son inherit the curses of his wicked father?

> *"If, however, he begets a son who sees all the sins which his father has done, and considers but does not do likewise; who has not eaten on the mountains, nor lifted his eyes to the idols of the house of Israel, nor defiled his neighbor's wife; has not oppressed anyone, nor withheld a pledge, nor robbed by violence, but has given his bread to the hungry and covered the naked with clothing; who has withdrawn his hand from the poor and not received usury or increase, but has executed My judgments and walked in My statutes—he shall not die for the iniquity of his father; he shall surely live!"* (Ezekiel 18:14–17)

What happens to the son who does not practise the sins of his father? He **does not receive** the curses of his father! He is rewarded with blessings. He is blessed for his good deeds and his obedience to God.

God is not evil! God is not man. People surmise and logically evaluate things by what they see. They assess things according to how they are in the natural, and by how much sense it makes to them. God does not think like man. In Isaiah we read, *"For My thoughts are not your thoughts, nor are your ways My ways,"* says the Lord. *"For as the heavens are higher than the earth, so are My ways higher than your ways, and My thoughts than your thoughts."* (Isaiah 55:8, 9)

Does God say that anywhere else? Let us take further back in the Old Testament. *"He is the Rock, His work is perfect; for all His ways are justice, a God of truth and without injustice; righteous and upright is He."* (Deuteronomy 32:4) All God's ways are just. Not all man's ways are just. As well, we can read in Revelation that God's ways are greater than man's. *"They sing the song of Moses, the servant of God, and the song of the Lamb, saying: "Great and marvelous are*

*Your works, Lord God Almighty! Just and true are Your ways, O King of the saints!"* (Revelation 15:3) We can now easily conclude that God's ways are higher than man's ways, and His ways are just, while man's ways can be unjust sometimes (by God's influence man can act justly). We thus have three portions of Scripture that testify to this truth.

While man with his limited and small thinking has brought God's thoughts down to his own level in his mind, God is still God. God does not reward people by giving them bad for good, or good for bad. He is wiser than that. That is not how God desires us to decipher His word! That is not how He would have us contemplate what He has said in the Bible. God wants us to interpret His Word with His Word. We can read it for ourselves. If someone tells us differently, we no longer have to believe them. This means that we should take the Bible ourselves, open it and read what God has to say. When we hear a preacher preach a sermon to us, we must look closely at how he interprets it, and check to see if it is in accordance with the Bible. When we receive a teaching from someone, we must make sure that the Scripture speaks the exact same thing two, three, or more times. We thus know better because of God's own words. We do not have to be so gullible that we believe everything that is taught us.

## Idol Worship

As we saw previously, 'a generational curse' was pronounced upon those who had turned from God to worship idols. Look at this again, *"You shall not make for yourself a carved image... you shall not bow down to them nor serve them. For I, the Lord your God, am a jealous God, visiting the iniquity of the fathers upon the children to the third and fourth generations of those who hate Me,"* (Exodus 20:4-5) That statement was not intended for or directed at all of Israel. It was spoken only against those who were worshipping idols. Pay attention to what God says to Ezekiel about the righteous son of an unrighteous father. *"...Nor lifted his eyes to the idols of the house of Israel..."* (Ezekiel 18:15) He is telling us that if this good son does not worship idols, but serves the living God, he will not inherit the curse of Exodus 20:5. He says, *"...He shall not die for the iniquity of his father; He shall surely live!"* (Ezekiel 18:1) Do you see the exclamation mark? God is serious about this. The righteous son does not have to pay for his father's iniquity.

## Repentance

Repentance is, though, a requirement for each and every one of us. *"Now therefore, amend your ways and your doings, and obey the voice of the Lord your God; then the Lord will relent concerning the doom that He has pronounced against you."* (Jeremiah 26:13) Then again,

> *"'But if a wicked man turns from all his sins which he has committed, keeps all My statutes, and does what is lawful and right... None of the transgressions which he has committed shall be remembered against him; because of the righteousness which he has done, he shall live. Do I have any pleasure at all that the wicked should die?' says the Lord God, 'and not that he should turn from his ways and live?'"* (Ezekiel 18:21–23)

It is still God's will that all be saved and that none perish. It is still God's desire to bless His people, and that evil would not come upon them. It is sad that God's people often believe that their God, as righteous and holy as He is, would permit the curses or punishment for their earthly father's sin, to pass on to them. It must terribly grieve God's heart that His people think that way.

God made the greatest sacrifice when He placed His only begotten Son, Jesus Christ the Messiah, upon a cross and let Him die for the sins of every person in the world. How could such a God allow the curses of their forefathers to come upon them? It is time that we give God the credit he is due. He is loving, kind, faithful and true, longsuffering, gentle, merciful and gracious... the list goes on and on. He is mighty, holy, wonderful, awesome and amazing. He is worthy of all our praises, adoration and love. "Yet you say, 'Why should the son not bear the guilt of the father?' Well, if *"the son does what is lawful and right, and has kept all My statutes and observed them, he shall surely live. The soul who sins shall die. The son shall not bear the guilt of the father, nor the father bear the guilt of the son. The righteousness of the righteous shall be upon himself, and the wickedness of the wicked shall be upon himself."* (Ezekiel 18:19) Why shouldn't the son bear, carry, take upon himself, pay for, and suffer the consequence of the sins of his father? Only because, he has not committed the evil acts of his father! It is as simple as that!

Right there, in the book of Ezekiel in the Old Testament, God changed the requirements of the law of Exodus 20:5, with regard to sons being responsible for the sins of their fathers.

> *"The Lord is long-suffering and slow to anger, and abundant in mercy and loving-kindness, forgiving iniquity and transgression; but He will by no means clear the guilty, visiting the iniquity of the fathers upon the children, upon the third and fourth generation."* (Numbers 14:18 AMP)

*'He will by no means clear the guilty'* means exactly what it says. The guilty will pay for their sins. And *'visiting the iniquity of the fathers'* -- *v*isiting simply means to punish. It signifies, therefore, that God brings punishment for the evil committed. The children up to the fourth generation were guilty by default because of Exodus 20:5. Therefore, in the past, before Ezekiel chapter 18, the children paid the price for their father's sins. They were punished for the sins of their fathers. This does not mean that the father's iniquity was passed on to the son as some people believe and teach. It signifies, therefore, that God brings punishment for the evil committed.

Since it is clear now that God is the One visiting, and God is holy and true, He does not pass on the sins of wicked fathers to their children and place it in their flesh. He punished the children down the line to the third and fourth generation for their father's sins. However, He ordered Ezekiel to put an end to it – it was finished. We have clearly seen that God *ended* this demand or requirement -- this 'generational curse' as it is called by so many. Even though, the Lord dealt with this and totally ended it; there are preachers, teachers and so called 'leaders' who are still forcing this untruth down the throats of many Christians. If this really bothers me; I can only imagine how it makes God feel…

They say that '*visiting the iniquity of the fathers upon the children, upon the third and fourth generation*' is the iniquity of the fathers passed on to the children. They say it is in their flesh. This is their explanation for someone who is a Christian, who is struggling with sin in their life. Can you believe that some people actually interpret God's Word this way? This is how some Bible scholars, preachers and teachers explain it, "It is the deep evil practices, iniquities of their fathers -- generational curses -- that have been passed on to them." This is their interpretation of '*God visiting iniquity*'. After all the Scripture verses that you have just read, can you believe that some people still preach and teach this fallacy -- this untruth?

In saying that, God has put the iniquities of the fathers upon their children, who are Christians, these people have totally blamed God for people's sinful practices. They have, in essence, put the responsibility of people's sins upon God. God help us! "Oh no, Pastor David, that is not what they say. They mean to say that iniquity is passed down from the father to the son or daughter, and the Christian person has to be delivered from the demon inside them who is causing them to practise sin." This sounds so true and believable doesn't it? Let us look at more facts.

First, the father's iniquity has not passed on to the Christian. The Lord has not taken the iniquity of the father and passed it on **to God's children**. That is who you are as a Christian, God's child. "*Therefore if the Son makes you free, you shall be free indeed.*" (John 8:36) Second, as a Christian, your Father is God so your inheritance is from God. I can thus guarantee you that God did not pass any iniquity or generational curse on to you. Third, the Holy Spirit will not live in the same house with a demon spirit. However, sin is sin and there is punishment for sin. That is the reason why Jesus Christ died. He Himself carried the punishment for our sins. We committed the crime, He did the time. We did wrong, and Jesus Christ who did no wrong, paid the full price for our evil deeds.

> "Yet you say, 'The way of the Lord is not fair.' Hear now, O house of Israel, is it not My way which is fair, and your ways which are not fair? When a righteous man turns away from his righteousness, commits iniquity, and dies in it, it is because of the iniquity which he has done that he dies." (Ezekiel 18:25, 26)

May I clarify another thing? If you are suffering some consequence of your own doing, do not put it on your fathers. You are being punished for your own sins. Repent of it! God is faithful to His Word and will forgive you. He will wash you with the blood of His Son, forget that you did wrong, deliver you from your situation, and bring blessings into your life. It might take time for everything to come back to a peaceful place, but God will do it.

> "Therefore I will judge you, O house of Israel, every one according to his ways,' says the Lord God. 'Repent, and turn from all your transgressions, so that iniquity will not be your ruin. Cast away from you all the transgressions which you have committed, and get yourselves a new heart and a new spirit. For why should you die, O house of Israel? For I have no pleasure in the death of one who dies,' says the Lord God. 'Therefore turn and live!'" (Ezekiel 18:29–32)

Sin is what separated Adam from God and thus separates the sinner from God. That is why Jesus died and rose again from the dead. He paid the price for our sins so that we do not have to pay for them. God will not punish you for your father's evil, nor for his evil practices, nor will He punish you for your past sins.

Get rid of any sin that is in your life. Turn to God. He will forgive you, and cleanse you of all of them. Get a new heart. Receive a new spirit from Him. The Book of John says, "*If we confess our sins, He is faithful and just to forgive us our sins and to cleanse us from all unrighteousness.*" (I John 1:9) and furthermore in Isaiah, "*I, even I, am He who blots out your transgressions for My own sake; and I will not remember your sins. Put Me in remembrance; let us contend together; state your case, that you may be acquitted.*" (Isaiah 43:25–26) When God blots out your sins, He does not hide them somewhere until He is ready to look at them again. "*As far as the east is from the west, He removes our transgressions from us.*" (Psalm 103:12) He totally erases them and forgets them. Your past sins will be gone from His memory! If there is no evidence of sin, there can be no payment for our sin. Why is that? Jesus Christ paid the full price for our sins.

"But Pastor, what if I did something that has brought a consequence that cannot change? For instance, bringing a child into this world outside of marriage?" You now have a great responsibility to carry don't you? Your duty is to nurture that child to the best of your ability. If you do not let God help you: you will not do the best job of raising that child. If you let Him assist you; He will do it through you. "*For it is God who works in you both to will and to do for His good pleasure.*" (Philippians 2:13)

> Dear Father God, You made the ultimate sacrifice in Jesus Christ my Lord and Saviour. You gave Him up to die here on the earth for me that I might live and not die and go to hell. You have a home prepared for me in Heaven and one day, I will spend eternity with You in bliss and harmony. I surrender to Your will and into Your hand. Greater is Your Spirit

in me than the devil who is in the world. By Your power and Your Holy Spirit, I will defeat sin and overcome all temptation because You will help me. You are my help and my strength, my hiding place and my strong defence. I will not be afraid, but trust in Your love for me and Your power to being me out of any and all difficulties. Sin will not rule my life. I ask you now Father to take full control of my life and to make it totally what you want it to be. I ask this in the name of Jesus Christ. Amen.

# 11

## BEGIN RIGHT

*"For the word of God is living and powerful,
and sharper than any two-edged sword...,
and is a discerner of the thoughts and intents
of the heart"*
(Hebrews 4:12)

I was twenty one years old. I was broken, distraught, depressed and oppressed. I had just come through the most terrible ordeal in my life and I was hurting really badly. I was attending church at the time, and I was also attending a prayer meeting every morning. However, I was still down and feeling bad about myself. I said to the Lord one day, "Lord, I need to study your Word, but in my condition I can't go to Bible College. Give me someone who will teach me on a one to one basis."

One day after an early morning prayer meeting at the Church I attended, a brother asked me if I had a job. I told him that I had been out of work for three months and was desperately seeking employment. He immediately called another brother, Peter Milec, and said to him, "Peter, we need to pray for a job for David."

"I don't need to pray for him." Peter paused. "I have a job for him if he wants it."

I accepted the job and began to work for him the next day. Peter saw my situation and the state of mind that I was in. He recognised that I was broken and depressed. Never, not once, though, did Peter ask me, "What's your problem? Why are you down? What happened?" Never! From the first day that I began to work for him, he fed me the Word of God. I sat in front of him at his desk every morning before I attended my duties, and he taught me. Day by day I changed.

Peter was legally blind so couldn't see to read. However, by listening to the Word of God on a cassette player, he had memorized the Bible in his heart. He taught the Bible using those tapes as well. By constantly listening to the Word of God, he had experienced a marvellous change in his own life. Therefore, he knew exactly what it would do to mine. As well, the Gideon New Testament on his desk was just waiting to be used. Every morning, I was asked to look in it for various passages of Scriptures, and to read them out loud. Every day for about two months, Peter taught me who I was in Christ and about the power I had in Christ. I learned what it really meant to be a new creation in Jesus.

This great mentor instilled in me the importance of worshipping the Lord while I worked, and to sing praises to Him, as well as to read the Bible as much as I could and whenever I could. He encouraged me to always pray to the Lord. He instructed me to also fast from time to time, fellowship with other Believers, attend church regularly, and give my tithes and offerings to God. He said that then my life would change. It did, much faster than I thought it would.

One day, about two months after I had started working for Peter, he sent someone to ask me to come to his office. Now, on my way to the office, I was concerned. "What had I done wrong? Where had I messed up? Had I failed to complete a job properly? – not done some duty that I was supposed to finish?" I was afraid that I might have failed somewhere. I entered Peter's office and stood before him, expecting him to scold me for a slip up. I thought that I had made a mistake somewhere or had left something undone.

Peter just asked me to sit down. "No, it's ok, I'll stand." I figured that I was going to take any correction standing up.

He proceeded to say, "David, do you remember the first time you came here how you were?"

I took a deep breath and sat down. So I hadn't done anything wrong. "I was right on the floor." I said to him.

He sat there with his arms crossed around his tummy, and chuckled. "No, you weren't. You were down in the basement looking up to see the bottom. Look at you now! Look at what Jesus has done for you. When you came here, if I asked you anything, you would say, 'Yes,' or 'No.' And you would look away. You couldn't look me in the eye. But, look at what Jesus has done for you."

My friend, Peter was not a psychologist, nor was he a trained counsellor. He was a man of God. All he had done was use the Word of God to transform my life. He never asked questions about my past life. He fed me God's Word and instructed me on a few important Biblical practices that would bring change in me, and in my life. He had left the rest to the Holy Spirit, who had completed the work of transformation.

Was I delivered from depression and demon oppression? Yes.

Was I freed from the pain and suffering I was going through? Yes.

Did I go through some 'generational curse' breaking ceremony? No.

Peter knew the power of the Word of God and he had used it. He knew full well,

> *"For the word of God is living and powerful, and sharper than any two-edged sword, piercing even to the division of soul and spirit, and of joints and marrow, and is a discerner of the thoughts and intents of the heart."* (Hebrews 4:12)

The Word of God is living, and it gives life. It will change any person who fills their heart and mind with it every day. Do not neglect it in your own life. Do not go without eating and drinking the Word of God on a daily basis. Your life will be beautifully transformed, and bountifully blessed if you are filled with it every day. *"It is the Spirit who gives life; the flesh profits nothing. The words that I speak to you are spirit, and they are life."* (John 6:63) Peter knew this, and he allowed God's Word to do its work in my heart and soul. It brought about change that remains not only to this day, but forever. God's Word will do the same for you if you fill your heart and mind with it every day.

## Don't Look Back

I am a changed man today because someone recognized who I am in Christ, and not who I was before Jesus saved me and came to live in my spirit. **He worked with what I am, and not with what I was.** You see, when we go back to the dead you, death is what we will find, death is what we will bring up, and death is what we will have in you. No wonder, God says, *"Do not remember the former things, nor consider the things of old."* (Isaiah 43:18) The Lord commanded us to forget the things of the past -- the memories of the past, the actions of the past, the desires and longings of the former person that we once were. We are commanded to forget the failures and shortcomings of the past as well as the hurt, the pain, and the disappointments of our past life. God wants us to stop looking back! He desires for us to look at today and to the future.

You begin to get freedom when you come to God in repentance. *"If we confess our sins, he is faithful and just to forgive us our sins, and to cleanse us from all unrighteousness."* (1 John 1:9) When you repent of your sins, transgressions and iniquities, and turn from them to serve God with a whole heart, the Lord will forgive you. He will forget your sins, transgressions and iniquities. He will cleanse you with the precious blood of Jesus Christ of all unrighteousness. The Bible says in Isaiah that, *"I, even I, am He who blots out your transgressions for My own sake; And I will not remember your sins."* (Isaiah 43:25) and again, *"I have blotted out, like a thick cloud, your transgressions, and like a cloud, your sins. Return to Me, for I have redeemed you."* (Isaiah 44:22) God has blotted out your sins, transgressions and iniquities, and He does not remember them anymore.

My prayer is that you would not desire to remember them either. Your past sins, transgressions, and iniquities belong to and are connected to the old person. If God has forgotten all of your old deeds; doesn't that mean that he has forgotten the old you as well? Now then, since that is true, why would you want to look back and remember? Why would you dig up the dead you who was buried with Christ? Why would you want to bring up from the grave, the dead you and your past sins, iniquities and transgressions? Then too, why would you allow anyone else to do so? *"Or do you not know that as many of us as were baptized into Christ Jesus were baptized into His death? Therefore we were buried with Him through baptism into death, that just as Christ was raised from the dead by the glory of the Father, even so we also should walk in newness of life."* (Romans 6:3, 4)

## Sin Must Be Dealt With

Therefore, you must not allow sin to remain in your life. You must not permit it to pull up a chair, sit down, and make itself as comfortable as another member of your family. You have to destroy it. You have to get rid of it. *"Thus says the Lord: 'Where is the certificate of your mother's divorce, whom I have put away? Or which of My creditors is it to whom I have sold you? For your iniquities you have sold yourselves, and for your transgressions your mother has been put away.'"* (Isaiah 50:1) Sin is what separates people from their God. It, therefore, must be destroyed and must be got rid of.

Nothing can separate us from the *love* God has for us. *"For I am persuaded that neither death nor life, nor* **angels nor principalities nor powers, nor things present nor things to come,** *nor height nor depth, nor any other created thing, shall be able to separate us from the love of God which is in Christ Jesus our Lord."* (Romans 8:38, 39) Think about it! God is love and He can only love. He doesn't hate and never will. He is, though, also a Judge and He judges righteously. What a person plants that is what he will also reap. So we read in John,

> *"Jesus answered them, I told you, and ye believed not: the works that I do in my Father's name, they bear witness of me. But ye believe not, because ye are not of my sheep, as I said unto you. My sheep hear my voice, and I know them, and they follow me: And I give unto them eternal life; and they shall never perish, neither shall any man pluck them out of my hand. My Father, which gave them me, is greater than all; and no man is able to pluck them out of my Father's hand. I and my Father are one."* (John 10:25-30)

## Where to Begin

Generational curses bring death and destruction. Jesus will never put, 'generational curses' or any such thing on you. He did not save you for that purpose. Therefore, you must start by getting rid of the old and beginning to do what is right and good. Notice that doing good, is learned. It is practised. It is what a person must train himself to do by first ceasing to do evil, and then by practicing the right thing. You have the responsibility to put away your wicked deeds. Another person cannot do it for you. It is your responsibility. In Isaiah, we read,

> *"Wash yourselves, make yourselves clean; put away the evil of your doings from before My eyes. Cease to do evil, learn to do good; seek justice, rebuke the oppressor; defend the fatherless, plead for the widow. 'Come now, and let us reason together,' says the Lord, though your sins are like scarlet, they shall be as white as snow; though they are red like crimson, they shall be as wool. If you are willing and obedient, you shall eat the good of the land."* (Isaiah 1:16-19)

You have to defeat sin in your life. You can, with the help of Holy Spirit, who will give you the strength, the power, and all that you need to do it, if you ask Him to. Again, *"Repent, and turn from all your transgressions, so that iniquity will not be your ruin."* (Ezekiel 18:30)

As a Christian, you have not been abandoned by God your Father. You are His child. Would He allow you to receive an inheritance from your past forefathers, especially, not a 'generational curse' that would destroy your life? The God that I serve loves you. He forgives. He cares. He is compassionate, merciful, faithful, kind, generous, and patient. He is not what so many people think that He is. He is not a destroyer. You have a new family, and you have a new Father. Your inheritance comes now from your new Father, God. **You are a new creation**. Would God, who loves you with an everlasting love, who gave His only begotten Son, Jesus Christ, to die for you, permit something from someone else's past to come over into your life to cause you harm? Is that the God you know and love? Is this how your loving Saviour who died on a cross because He loves you, act toward you? Would Jesus Christ simply allow curses from your forefathers to come into your life, after He bought you by paying the full price for you? After He saved you, washed you with His own blood from all your past sins? Is this the same Jesus Christ who loves the entire world so much that he died for them?

If you were God, would you permit, 'generational curses' to come over from forefathers into your child's life? Only the enemy comes to steal, kill and destroy –not God. "*The thief does not come except to steal, and to kill, and to destroy...*" (John 10:10) Satan comes and seeks to steal from you, and to destroy you. He will do everything possible to rob you, to steal your peace and joy, health and happiness; to deceive you, to bring you into bondage, and to have you remain there. If that means that he must make you believe that you have 'generational curses' all over your life, then he will lie to you, trick you, and deceive you to believe exactly that. According to how you believe, you will have. (Mark 11:23, 24)

On the other hand, Jesus came to give life to you, not death. He came to bless you, not rob you; to deliver you, not to place you in bondage. He saved you to make your life happy, not sad; to give you hope and a future.... "*I have come that they may have life, and that they may have it more abundantly.*" (John 10:10) and "*For I know the thoughts that I think toward you, says the Lord, thoughts of peace and not of evil, to give you a future and a hope.*" (Jeremiah 29:11)

> *Dear God, my Father, You will never abandon me not in bad times and, especially, not in good times. You are with me always. Your desire for me is good. It is to give me good things and not evil. I believe Your words in Jeremiah 29:11 that tell me that You want me to have 'a future without harm, with peace and happiness'. According to Isaiah 65:24, You answer my prayers before I say them to You and You hear me when I speak to You. Therefore Father, hear me now and deliver me from every evil, from trouble seen and unseen, from disasters that*

the enemy may plan for me, and from every works of Satan. I am Your child, Father, so please make all things good for me in every area of my life. I thank You Dear God, in Jesus' name. Amen.

# 12

## ACCORDING TO YOUR FAITH

*"… God hath dealt to every man the measure*
*of faith."*
(Romans 12:3)

What does all of this need? Faith… Faith moves mountains. Faith makes you whole. Faith makes you well. Faith heals the sick. Faith opens blind eyes. Faith raises the dead. Faith casts out demons. Faith brings the dead back to life. *"Faith is the substance of things hoped for, the evidence of things not seen."* (Hebrews 11:1) However, it is not faith in 'faith' itself that does all of this. It is faith in Jesus Christ and in His Word. When you walk by faith, great things are accomplished. When you are operating in faith, miracles happen. The Word says, *"Without faith it is impossible to please God."* (Hebrews 11:6) Look at the following all done by faith:

> *"Then He touched their eyes, saying, 'According to*
> *your faith let it be to you.'"* (Matthew 9:29)

*"And He said to her, 'Daughter, your faith has made you well. Go in peace, and be healed of your affliction.'"* (Mark 5:34)

*"Then Jesus said to him, 'Go your way; your faith has made you well.' And immediately he received his sight and followed Jesus on the road."* (Mark 10:52)

*"Then He said to the woman, 'Your faith has saved you. Go in peace.'"* (Luke 7:50)

You must have faith that God will remove all your sins and iniquities and make you born again. You must have faith that He can and will remove any curses from you.

You can do all things yourself well and good, but if you do not do them with faith, you have not pleased God and you will not see miracles. You can work extremely hard at what you do, and still not accomplish in life what you desire to accomplish. However, when you do what you do with faith, you please God. And when you please God, great things happen. Check out what proverbs says, *"When a man's ways please the Lord, He makes even his enemies to be at peace with him."* (Proverbs 16:7)

Faith does not grow on trees, though, neither is it found in mountains. It cannot be brought up from the sea, nor can it be dished out on a plate. It is not served on a platter in restaurants; neither can you buy it in a drugstore or any other store for that matter. Faith is only found in one place. It is found in God and in His Word. For His Word is *"living and powerful, and sharper than any two-edged sword, piercing even to the division of soul and spirit…."* (Hebrews 4:12)

If you desire to have greater faith you must go to God and ask for it. If you want to have more faith you must go to God's Word to increase it. Faith is given by God and faith grows. Your faith can grow. Further to this, *"And the apostles said to the Lord, 'increase our faith.' So the Lord said, 'If you have faith as a mustard seed, you can say to this mulberry tree, 'Be pulled up by the roots and be planted in the sea,' and it would obey you.'"* (Luke 17:5, 6) Jesus made sure that his disciples understood the first simple fundamental truth about faith. You do not need to have great faith to do great things. You can start with a mustard seed amount. You do not have to have plenty of faith. You can work with what you have. All it takes is a tiny bit, as much as the size of a grain of sand, which is about the size of a mustard seed. That much faith can move 'mountains' in your life. When you start with that much faith, and begin to move away 'mountains', that same 'mustard seed' faith can grow into the size of a mountain. So why wait to build your faith? Why not begin now and use the little bit of faith that you have, to get from God what you want and need?

## Sin Condemns

Whether your faith is as large as a mountain or as tiny as a seed, what can hinder it? Sin! Sin comes between you and God. When you sin, and even after you have repented, guilty feelings can still nag at you. Sin only brings you down and brings guilt and condemnation. It causes you to run from God, instead of running to Him. Sin causes you to not trust God. It makes you feel that you do not deserve anything from the Lord. It is what would destroy your faith.

If you feel guilty about any sin that you have committed; you are not going to believe that God is going to come through for you. You are going to walk around with your head hanging down, dragging your feet about, and having a pity party wherever you go. You will believe that God will do nothing for you because of the wrongs you have done.

Guilt and condemnation hang on and cling to you like a dirty rag. Unless you come into the presence of God; whether in a Holy Ghost meeting in your church or in a time of repentance and breaking before God in your own private place, guilt will hang around, and condemnation will choke you. When you have repented with your heart and experience that release and freedom from sin, then you will find that guilt and condemnation leave. You will feel that you can trust God again and you can believe Him to come through for you. That is the time when you should throw all your needs into one heap before God, and request that those needs be met! One by one, lay them before Him.

## The 'Faith Connection'

Do you ever wonder why it is that there are times when you go into prayer, and it seems to take so long before you know that you have made 'the connection' with God? What connection is that? It is called the 'Faith Connection.' Why is this so? It is because of what we have been discussing throughout this entire book. The enemy never lets up in his attempt to bring condemnation upon you. He never stops trying to make you feel guilty. He will always try to tempt you in order to bring you into bondage.

"Did you see how you looked at that beggar at the street corner today? What about the guy who cut you off on your way here? Do you remember being so upset at your wife because she was late packing your lunch, and caused you to leave late for work? How about the few extra minutes that you spent in the lunch room yesterday?" Well, you get the point. Satan never stops trying to interfere, interrupt, disrupt or hinder your faith. That is why you have to constantly make sure that your faith is always growing and not diminishing.

Maybe now, you will be able to understand why sometimes things do not seem to happen for you, even though, you have spent so much time praying for them to happen. Perhaps, it did not happen for you because you did not truly believe that God would do it for you. There were times, maybe, when you did not even believe that He wanted to do whatever you were asking for. Believe therefore, and you will see God work miracles in your life. Believe and there will not be one curse upon you. Believe and God will deliver you from them all. Live a life of obedience and holiness, seek intimacy with God, and your life will never be the same again. You will enjoy greater joy, peace and happiness. Remember, it is a life of faith, not works. Here is a great prayer for you:

*Father God, You have given me the measure of faith that I need to live a productive and fruitful life to Your honour and glory. I ask that my faith would grow as I read Your word on a daily basis, and that it would become more and more evident in me. The truth is that "I can do all things through Jesus who strengthens me" (Philippians 4:13) and Psalm 27:1 says "that the Lord is the strength of my life", therefore, strengthen my faith I pray, in the name of Jesus Christ. Amen.*

# 13

## IN CONCLUSION, THEN...
### (ECCLESIASTES 12:13)

*"Let us hear the conclusion of the whole matter:*
*Fear God, and keep his commandments: for this*
*is the whole duty of man."*

As you have followed this writing carefully, you have seen how God annulled the curses of Exodus 20:5. According to Ezekiel in chapter 18, GOD DECLARED THE CURSES AS **NULL** AND **VOID**. THEREFORE, WE **NO LONGER HAVE TO CONTEND** WITH THEM. WE are NOW UNDER A TRULY NEW COVENANT -- a covenant of GRACE and MERCY, FORGIVENESS and ACCEPTANCE, and NEWNESS OF LIFE IN ABUNDANCE. With this covenant, God made the ultimate sacrifice with Jesus Christ our Lord, so you and I accept His gift of salvation through Jesus and He accepts us. Under the Old Covenant, man made a sacrifice to God. If he did it sincerely from his heart; God accepted his sacrifice and also accepted the man. Truly old things have passed away and all things have become new.

\* \* \*

It has been raining for days. It has been wet, dark and dreary. Depressing comes to mind. It is the kind of weather that makes one sleep for hours. You have been sleeping, but then you awoke. It is morning and the sun is brightly shining. The trees shimmer and the grass is greener than ever before. Everything appears more brilliant and more beautiful than ever. The roses are redder and richer in color. The flowers are pure and perfumed. The air is filled with their perfume and the earth seems to be joyous. Your feet want to dance. Oh, how marvelous.... How wonderful. It is a new day. It is a new beginning. It is a new life. Breathe... Ahhhhhh...

You have been born again. You have a new life. You have been washed in the blood of Jesus Christ and you have been made clean. You have risen from the dead in Him and live to glorify His name. Translated into His marvelous light, you have moved into His Kingdom and now live in His house. Adopted into His family, you have become a child of Almighty God. He calls you son. You call Him Father.

Right from the very start, He made you His righteousness in Christ Jesus. You stand before Him justified as if you have done no wrong because He has accepted you in His Beloved Son. He sees you through Jesus because you are seated with Him next to God your Father in Heaven. You have been (are) still '*hidden in Him*' as '*He lives and moves and works*' in and through you. He makes you strong and able to do all things through Himself. There is nothing too difficult that He cannot do for you as He, Himself, is acquainted with any grief or sorrow that you may have experienced. He knows the pain you feel or the hardship you go through. Nothing escapes Him. Jesus sees all things.

> "*But God, who is rich in mercy, because of His great love with which He loved us, even when we were dead in trespasses, made us alive together with Christ (by grace you have been saved), and raised us*

*up together, and made us sit together in the heavenly*
*places in Christ Jesus."* (Ephesians 2:4-6)

As He lives in you, you can say, *"Greater is He in me* than the devil who is out there in the world. I am a champion, a winner, an overcomer. Since Jesus overcame the world I do too." The stage is set. The outcome has been written. You have been made an ambassador of Christ. You represent Him here on this earth. Wherever you go and whomever you encounter, you are a representative of God Almighty. If you were to sign on the dotted line, it would be as if Jesus Himself had signed. Can anything beat that? You have full representation -- full signing authority, and total power to do as He would here on earth.

However, God was not satisfied with only making you His ambassador; He made you a king. Kings rule and reign. They make declarations that cannot be changed or erased. Their words are final. You must speak out and declare what you know, but be careful what you say because once it leaves your lips, it cannot be taken back. *"But let your communication be, Yea, yea; Nay, nay: for whatsoever is more than these cometh of evil."* (Matthew 5:37) Your words go out to perform and accomplish whatever you said. (Proverbs 13:2; 18:21) Therefore, stick to the Word of God and you will not go wrong.

You are a king with God-given authority and power to rule and reign on this earth, especially, against the forces of the devil. Therefore, rule and reign. Declare what God has said about you. Proclaim His promises over your life and speak His words of healing and blessing. Then, stand back and watch God perform His words in your life such as you have never seen before. All that God desires for you to do is to agree with what He has said, believe it and speak it, and He will make it happen for you. He is ready, willing and able to do more for you than *"you can ask, think or imagine".* (Ephesians 3:20) It is written that God fulfills His promises and that He also performs the words of His servants. *"Who confirms the word of His servant, and performs the counsel of His messengers."* (Isaiah 44:26)

We also see the confirmation in Paul's writings. *"And being fully convinced that what He had promised He was also able to perform."* (Romans 4:21)

The Lord did not stop at kingship. He wants you to be able to come before Him with your offerings as the Old Testament priests used to do. Therefore, He made you a priest. Your offerings of praise, your songs of worship, your dance and the lifting of your hands, your laughter and your thanksgiving -- all rise to the Lord as a sweet smelling perfume that delights the heart of God. Your tithes and your offerings that you give freely from your heart with gratitude and thankfulness, your time and labour in the Kingdom of God, your love and care for other Christians, your respect for God's house, the respect and honor you show to those in authority over you in Gods' Kingdom -- everything you do for Him rises to *the Lord as an accepted sacrifice on the altar of God.*

> *"And they sang a new song, saying: 'You are worthy to take the scroll, and to open its seals; for You were slain, and have redeemed us to God by Your blood out of every tribe and tongue and people and nation, and have made us kings and priests to our God; and we shall reign on the earth.'"* (Revelation 5:9-10)

No wonder He calls you holy, acceptable, beloved, honored, favored, righteous and royal. You are privileged and have the honor of serving God. He has bestowed that upon you and granted you to have an inheritance from Him in Jesus Christ. You are truly richer than you know -- a spiritual giant, a powerhouse, and a force to be considered and respected. Glad to be your brother. J

> *"Blessed be the God and Father of our Lord Jesus Christ, who has blessed us with every spiritual blessing in the heavenly places in Christ, just as He chose us in Him before the foundation of the world, that we should be holy and without blame before Him in love, having predestined us to adoption as*

*sons by Jesus Christ to Himself, according to the good pleasure of His will, to the praise of the glory of His grace, by which He made us accepted in the Beloved. In Him we have redemption through His blood, the forgiveness of sins, according to the riches of His grace. In Him also we have obtained an inheritance, being predestined according to the purpose of Him who works all things according to the counsel of His will, that we who first trusted in Christ should be to the praise of His glory.*"
(Ephesians 1:3-7; 11-12)

There is now no condemnation for you who are in Christ and who are being led by the Holy Spirit. You crossed the threshold when you became a new creation. All things became new — the old you passed away. You are brand new in God's new world His Kingdom. You have been empowered to live a full and free life for Him and in Him. '*Come into His presence with thanksgiving*' and bring an offering. '*Serve Him with gladness*', serve Him with passion, serve Him with vigor, and serve Him with a fire burning in your soul to see His glory come upon the earth, and to see men and women, boys and girls everywhere coming to know and accept Him as Lord and Saviour. The bottom line of all is in Ecclesiastes 12:13: "*Let us hear the conclusion of the whole matter: Fear God, and keep his commandments: for this is the whole duty of man.*"

Stand firm therefore in this freedom you have received in Jesus. You are truly free.

God bless you.

*"But seek first the Kingdom of*
*God and His righteousness, and all*
*these things shall be added to you."*
*(Matthew 6:33)*

*Alleluia!*

If this book has blessed you, please share your testimony. Follow
him at :

Email: mail@christexaltedministries.com www.
christexaltedministries.com

https://ccmfcanada.org/ https://www.facebook.com/david.ramiah

https://twitter.com/DavidRamiah

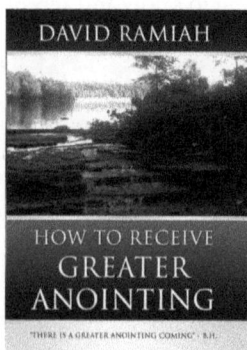

DAVID RAMIAH

HOW TO RECEIVE
GREATER
ANOINTING

"THERE IS A GREATER ANOINTING COMING" - B.H.

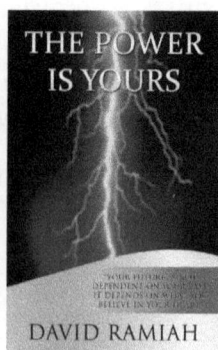

THE POWER
IS YOURS

"YOUR VICTORY IS NOT
DEPENDENT ON YOU-IT
IT DEPENDS ON WHO YOU
BELIEVE IN-YOU..."

DAVID RAMIAH

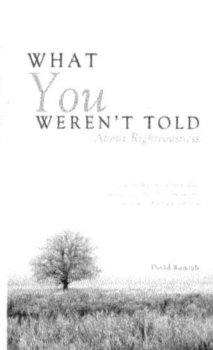

WHAT
*You*
WEREN'T TOLD
*About Righteousness*

David Ramiah